For permission requests, speaking inquiries, corporate sponsorship, bulk orders, and purchase options, email: info@globalgirlsglow.org

Produced by Diamond Queen, LLC and Dr. Izdihar Jamil, Ph.D.
Cover by Hunain Arshad.
Edited by Ginger Harris.

Featuring:
Anu Jain | Crystal Sprague | Gerardo Porteny Backal | Dr. Izdihar Jamil | Jennie Blumenthal | Joy Donnell | Kelsey Chittick | Kylie Van Luyn | Kylie Schuyler | Laura Probst | Dr. Lindsay Ruiz | Mamta Valderrama | Meera Gandhi | Dr. Michele Goodwin | Nandini Sankara | Shruthi Kumar

Youth Authors:
Jada Renée | Inioluwa | Huong

Disclaimer:
The authors in no way, shape, or form consider any of the information in this book to be a promise, guarantee, warranty, or any form of professional advice. It is intended for informational and educational purposes only. The results produced by the authors, or anyone referenced in the book, are mentioned for illustration purposes only and are not intended to imply or suggest that you will have results that are similar to those in the book.

ISBN: 979-8-9925389-1-5 (Paperback)
ISBN: 979-8-9925389-0-8 (EPUB)

VOICES
For
IMPACT

How to Unapologetically Share Your Message With
Courage, Clarity and Compassion

Featuring:

Brave Women From Diverse
Backgrounds

Table of Contents

Foreword

The thing I admire most about artists is how they delight in their own uniqueness and are unbelievably devoted to discovering their own voices. The most vital part of being an artist is being connected to what you want to say. It's the beginning of everything. There is no potential for sustenance, entertainment or impact without first knowing what it is your unique instrument is here to articulate. I'm grateful that as a first generation Cuban-American, I was drawn to the courage of a creative life and was supported by my community to connect to and strengthen my voice. But while I love this creative world, I simultaneously have one foot in this other place. A place of cultural relics that don't service us, where women and girls are encouraged to shrink. I see that place and it reminds me why this book is so important.

The biggest lesson I've learned from using my voice is that it doesn't have to be some huge thing, broadcast to millions. I've found that the seemingly smallest consistent use of my voice has the most profound impacts. When I have spoken for things that affect my immediate community or when I've made the people directly around me *feel*, I have seen responses and results I never thought possible. Don't be tempted to give up your power prematurely and don't think that everything has already been said. What you have to say is different and meaningful to your community because it comes from you.

When you practice using your voice, you gain greater control and power over your life, so you can make better informed decisions about your health, education, and future. I was moved to work with Global Girls Glow because I saw the way young women were learning to use their voices and power to advocate for change that they believe in. Just like you intend to. And maybe you're looking for guidance or permission to use your voice more confidently. I know how intimidating it can feel, I know the tactics "the others" deploy to discourage you from using that beautiful voice of yours.

I want to encourage you to *run towards feeling*, not away. That rush bubbling up in your chest, that's where we go from here on out. We go towards that and we steady ourselves with the reminder that we are not alone. We are a part of a legacy of women who have stood right in this same place of fullness and anticipation and those women steadied their voices. And because they did, you and I are here right now in this moment. So now it's your turn. And you are at the perfect place to start. See you on the other side. Thanks for what you're doing.

Jeanine Mason
Actress, Dancer, and Advocate

Introduction

I was checking my email at Mama's dining table in Malaysia when I noticed a message from Laura Probst. I didn't recognize the name, but judging by the subject line, I assumed it was another pitch for a TEDx talk.

As the Curator for TEDxHuntingtonBeach, I get emails like this almost daily. Nine out of ten are generic marketing pitches, rarely focused on connection or building relationships.

Every summer, my kids and I spend time in Malaysia, where I'm originally from. It's our opportunity to reconnect with family and culture. During these "mini-retirements," the last thing I want to do is respond to TEDx pitches.

But something about Laura's email pulled me in. She introduced herself as part of Global Girls Glow, a non-profit mentoring girls around the world to become confident leaders and powerful advocates for themselves and others. Their signature program, GLOW Club, operates in over 30 countries, offering girls a safe space to speak up, build confidence, and stand for causes they believe in.

Laura's email stood out—not because of its structure, but because of the passion, warmth, and commitment behind her words. It didn't feel like a typical pitch for fame or glory. Instead, it felt like an invitation to expand an important mission.

Reading about Global Girls Glow reminded me of my ten-year-old daughter, Nadrah. Laura's words painted a vision of what's possible for girls like her and others everywhere. That personal connection moved me to respond, thanking Laura and asking a few questions about her vision and the organization.

Her genuine replies led to a call, right there at Mama's kitchen table. Laura was warm, nurturing, and deeply committed to her mission. Inspired, I offered to host a short "Ask Us Anything" session for her organization's members and aspiring speakers, sharing lessons I've learned as a TEDx speaker and curator.

After that session and meeting the incredible people behind the organization, I felt even more aligned with Global Girls Glow. They're not just an organization—they're a heart-based movement creating platforms for girls and women to share their voices, even in the face of immense challenges. Shortly after, Laura invited me to speak at their event, *A Conversation About Inclusive Storytelling and Representation for Gender, Culture, and Youth*, celebrating International Day of the Girl at the Loreal ProLab in Los Angeles.

The invitation to that event sparked an idea: a book to amplify the voices of girls and women. I envisioned something tangible that attendees could take home—a book carrying the hearts and stories of brave individuals that would inspire its readers to tell their stories, too.

The thought of creating a lasting legacy filled me with purpose. A book showcasing diverse voices and impactful stories felt like the perfect way to honor Global Girls Glow's mission while offering a gift of hope and light to readers worldwide.

With that vision, I mustered the courage to propose the idea to Laura. My inner doubts whispered, *"They are going to say no. Why would they work with you? They are not going to be interested."*. But I reminded myself that my role is to serve as a vessel, offering this opportunity without fear of judgment.

And that's how the book, *Voices for Impact: How to Share Your Message with Courage, Clarity, and Compassion*, was born!

This anthology brings together authors who share the Global Girls Glow vision: empowering girls and women to use their voices to create change. This book is more than a collection of inspiring stories—it's packed with practical tips, lessons, and actionable steps to help you share your message with courage, clarity, and compassion.

Pamela G. Bradley, the singer/songwriter and bestselling author of *Women Who Trust*, had an early glimpse of the book, and said:

"What a beautiful collection of personal stories that not only instill hope for our next generation of leaders but give them, and you, powerful takeaways and actionable steps to stand out in a noisy world with your message for change."

Inside these pages, you'll find stories of girls and women overcoming hardships like discrimination, loss of a spouse, and childhood trauma. In each one, the author not only found a way to survive but thrive, breaking barriers and harnessing the power of their inner voice. Here's a sneak peak at the chapters:

My Daughter Priyanka: A Journey of Passion and Discovery: Anu Jain shares how motherhood and pushing boundaries helped her inspire her daughter to dream bigger. Her chapter highlights the joy of encouraging children to explore passions beyond their comfort zones and the transformative power of thinking big.

Why Do Men Benefit from Gender Equality?: Gerardo Porteny Backal explores how gender equality benefits everyone, including men. His chapter highlights the importance of collaboration, education, and engaging men as allies to break stereotypes and foster a thriving, inclusive society.

How I Lost My Voice in the Hustle—and Found It Again: Jennie Blumenthal explores the courage it takes to break free from people-pleasing and embrace vulnerability. Her chapter shows how sharing unpolished truths can lead to personal freedom and inspire others to find and use their voices.

A Fire Starts to Burn: Joy Donnell reveals how reclaiming her story gave her the strength to own her voice and inspire others. Her chapter highlights the power of speaking the truth, embracing authenticity, and finding the courage to stand for what's right—even when it burns.

The Magic in the Missing: Kelsey Chittick shares her journey of transforming grief into gratitude and resilience. Her chapter inspires readers to embrace life's hardships as opportunities for growth, teaching the power of bravery and trust in life's bigger plan.

Girls Scout, Boys Dig: How I Learned to Choose Courage: Kylie Schuyler, PhD shares how a single moment opened her eyes to the limitations placed on girls. Her chapter explores the power of self-acceptance, emotional courage, and bold action, inspiring readers to challenge societal expectations and step into their own strength.

From Blending In to Inspiring Change: Kylie van Luyn reveals how overcoming imposter syndrome allowed her to create legislative and social change for women and girls. Her chapter reminds readers that every girl has the power to rewrite her story and inspire meaningful change.

Saying 'No' to an 'Easy Yes': Laura Probst shows how trusting her instincts and embracing uncertainty led her to a fulfilling career and life. Her chapter encourages readers to make bold, authentic decisions that align with their values and passions.

When Words Fail You: Dr. Lindsay Ruiz reveals how speaking up for what's right, even imperfectly, can create ripples of change. Her chapter emphasizes using your voice as a powerful tool for justice, connection, and transformation, even when the steps feel small.

We Can Do Hard Things: Mamta Jain Valderrama highlights how small acts of encouragement can inspire confidence and create ripples of change. Her chapter shares how teaching her daughter to face challenges empowered multiple generations to believe in their potential.

Three Tips on Reconciliation: Meera Gandhi shares a heartfelt story of how compassion, forgiveness, and empathy transformed a moment of conflict into a lifelong bond. Her chapter highlights the liberating power of reconciliation and the unexpected joy it can bring, inspiring readers to embrace unity and understanding in their own lives.

Standing In One's Power: Paying Homage to Our Foremothers: **Dr. Michele Goodwin** reflects on the resilience of women who fought for democracy, civil rights, and gender equality. Her chapter honors the quiet strength of generations before us and the transformative power of writing, reminding us that standing in our power is both a privilege and a responsibility.

From Dreams to Action: My Transformative Journey: Nandini Sankara reflects on her journey from Mumbai to leadership in the energy sector. Her chapter emphasizes resilience, courage, and the importance of giving back, inspiring readers to embrace challenges and lead with purpose.

Step Up and Step Back: Shruthi Kumar shares a deeply personal journey of navigating cultural norms and challenging inequities with empathy and patience. Her chapter highlights the importance of meaningful conversations, embracing complexity, and finding common ground to create lasting change across generations.

We can't wait for you to dive into these stories and ideas. Here's to sharing your voice and making an impact!

With love and gratitude,

Dr. Izdihar Jamil, Ph.D.
Curator and Producer of *Voices for Impact*
Bestselling Author | TEDx Curator | TV Show Host
www.izdiharjamil.com

JADA'S STORY

Reclaiming My Reflection

Hello! My name is Jada Hill. I'm seventeen years old, and I'm from the United States of America.

I'm a Leo—confident, self-assured, and outspoken. At least, that's what they say. The truth is, it took me years to begin to find my voice, to summon the courage to speak my mind and stand in my own light. My mother always told me I was enough, that I was beautiful just as I am. Yet words, no matter how kind, can only echo so far when you don't believe them.

I grew up feeling like I didn't belong. My parents believed in private schools, thinking they offered the best education, but that choice left me surrounded by faces that didn't look like mine. I was the only one—different, noticeable, exposed. I remember sixth grade vividly, a time when I wore my hair in puffs and afros, bold and full of life. To me, my hair was beautiful, a crown.

But to others, my hair was an anomaly. White girls would ask to touch it, fascinated by how "different" it was, while others looked at it with judgment, calling it "too much." Their stares and whispers wrapped around me, tighter than I realized, until I found myself reaching for a flat iron more often than not—smoothing myself out, blending in, dimming my light.

Even when teachers crossed lines, saying things that should have made me angry, I stayed silent. I had learned to let things slide, to brush off the slurs and the stares because I didn't think my voice would make a difference. The mirror became my quiet enemy. I'd look into it and see someone I didn't recognize—someone muted, trying hard to be anyone but herself.

At the time, I didn't realize how much I was giving away—how much of myself I was hiding just to fit in. The world made me feel like I was too much and not enough, all at the same time. I stopped loving the parts of myself that made me who I was. My hair, my skin, my voice—things I once held with pride—felt more like burdens than blessings.

Then the world stopped. COVID came, and while it brought pain and uncertainty, it also brought quiet. For the first time in years, I wasn't surrounded by the noise of other people's opinions. I

was alone with myself, forced to confront the person I had become. It was uncomfortable at first, even painful, but it was also the beginning of something beautiful.

During those months of stillness, I started to reflect. Piece by piece, I began to reclaim the parts of me I had tucked away for the comfort of others. For far too long, I assimilated to my surroundings, hiding my true self.

I rediscovered the joy in embracing my identity, no longer feeling the need to shrink myself to fit into spaces that were never meant to contain me. It was a slow process—unraveling years of self-doubt, unlearning the belief that my features needed to be subdued to be acceptable. I spent time relearning the beauty in my reflection, in the rich depth of my skin, in the tight coils that framed my face. Each day, I grew more comfortable in my authenticity, shedding the fear that once held me captive.

I started to wear my afros and puffs again, unapologetically. I looked at my skin and saw beauty, not inconvenience. I can recall detangling my coiled hair and watching the conditioner go through each coil. I can recall how tired my hand was from styling my natural hair again—a feeling that I missed. For the first time in years, I felt whole. When my mother saw me wearing my natural hair again, she was in shock.

"Look at you! Finally deciding to take my advice. I always told you that you were enough and not to dim your light for others." Her words stayed with me, echoing in my mind as I looked at myself in the mirror. It wasn't just about hair; it was about seeing myself for who I truly was and knowing I no longer had to hide.

Opportunities like Global Girls Glow remind me of how far I've come. This program helped me find my voice and use it to make an impact. Through sharing my story, I've learned that my voice matters—not just for others, but for me, too. Silence, I've realized, can hide you, but speaking your truth sets you free. Now, I see my voice as a gift—a way to inspire and uplift others. Global

Girls Glow taught me that when you share your light, you empower others to find theirs. And that's a legacy I'm proud to continue.

My advice for other girls is to discover your voice through self-reflection, start with small steps, and surround yourself with supportive people. Embrace your values, and know that your voice can inspire change.

STANDING IN ONE'S POWER

Dr. Michele Goodwin
Author | Executive Producer

---✦---

"Be strong, be fearless, be beautiful. And believe that anything is possible when you have the right people there to support you." — Misty Copeland

---✦---

What does it mean to stand in one's power? Over the years, significant opportunities to positively impact people's lives around the world have been part of my journey. From advising the White House on matters of national and global importance in women's lives to testifying before Congress and state legislatures, the ability to use my voice as a platform for positive change has been a source of power and strength. And, because my work is both national and global, the ability to work cross-culturally and collaborate with researchers, writers, civil society members, professors, judges, and lawmakers around the world is a privilege for which I am grateful. Recently, my daughter and I calculated that I have traveled to nearly 50 countries to collaborate, research, and lecture.

For me, to stand in one's power includes holding grace, integrity, accountability, dignity, perseverance, and courage in balance. In my life, standing in power is a history-bridging exercise that uplifts women rendered invisible by their circumstances—be it race, sex, geography, religion, or economic insecurity. Each day, in some way, I pay homage to the women who refused to surrender their seats at lunch counters or on buses. The women who dared to walk through the front doors of department stores and restaurants even when doing so might be met with reprimand or law enforcement involvement. I am moved by women who demanded voting rights and risked sacrificing their employment and housing security and exposed themselves to arrest and incarceration to pursue the quest for democracy.

I marvel at the fortitude, tenacity, and strength of courage found in women who sought to elevate from a deeply embedded second-class citizenship. Only a generation or two ago, married women had to petition to have credit cards and checking accounts in their own name, and the legacy of women being denied service on juries or having to affirmatively petition to serve was not that long ago. More and more, I reflect on the insufficiently sung dynamic women who brilliantly charted frameworks for democracy. Ms. Lucille Bridges—the brave mother of Rugy Bridges—comes to mind.

The Lesson

To understand the bravery and reach of Lucille Bridges, Fannie Lou Hamer, Pauli Murray, Ida B. Wells, and other Black women of their generation is to appreciate their tenacity, indefatigability, unwavering sense of justice, and their remarkable impacts on society. Although unsung, they remarkably took action despite the risks of speaking up. Notably, their work was not only for themselves or the communities from which they came. They believed that women deserved to be heard, valued, and taken seriously.

For me, I draw lessons from foremothers. Those foremothers who are biologically related as well as women who I admire, but have no familial connections are beacons of hope and light. I read Fannie Lou Hamer's enduring statement: "Nobody's free until everybody's free," as a test of constitutional meaning and value. *Can a constitution have meaning if it has no effect? Can equality exist if women are excluded? Can women achieve liberty if some women are excluded based on race, sexual orientation, or religion?*

For these reasons, standing in power is personal and professional—and one is not disconnected from the other in my life. My grandmothers were the foundational seeds of my blossoming. They taught me that power, integrity, accountability, and dignity are lived values. They are practiced. As a law professor, this continues to resonate with me.

The benefit of growing up as I did, sharing time between both sets of grandparents, was that family was presented as an entity that is loving, caring, and not bound by genetics and biology. Love is open, honest, and joyful. I was fortunate to have that as my founding story, especially as I am keenly aware of the fragility of family bonds and relationships.

I felt the deep, unconditional, and unshakeable love of my grandmothers in my early, foundational years with my grandmothers. With them, I felt the warmth of possibilities and joy. In my work, I continue to embrace the profound lessons of joy as an antidote. I understand it as a salve and form of resistance and defiance. From this perspective, there is so much power in the adage carried by Black women in an African American tradition: "Don't let anyone steal your joy."

The Understanding

To understand the powers of joy and resistance is at least to acknowledge that one of my grandmothers was the offspring of America's Jim Crow legal system. It was a legal structure that denied voting rights, educational opportunities, equality in housing, fairness in lending, and shamefully even banned Black children from enjoying amusement in parks and swimming pools. Without the 1964 Civil Rights Act, 1965 Voting Rights Act, and landmark civil rights cases this system would likely have endured for decades to come.

Yet, when I think about what allows someone to survive beyond a system so inhuman and denigrating, I'm reminded of much there is yet to learn from women who have been left out of our national narratives. I learned from my grandmothers that one could convey and teach without speaking. That love could be communicated in subtle ways, every day: the grasp of a hand, the look in the eye, gardening, and even being given the spoon that whipped the cream for the cake. However, their love also included teaching me to read and write. Indeed, my earliest memories include sitting on the lap of my maternal grandmother while she read to me.

Today, I am a professor of law, and I have the privilege of holding a prestigious, endowed chair at a prominent university. I am also the executive producer of *Ms. Studios*—the audio and visual arm of *Ms.* magazine, which was launched by Gloria Steinem in 1972 and an extraordinary group of thoughtful, courageous women. My articles are assigned to classes around the world, and I have the honor to share my perspectives on law, policy, women's rights, and health around the world. Yet, I am keenly aware that my "start" began with my grandmothers. Even today, I have fond memories of my "Little Golden Books" with their prominent gold spines depicting flowers, bees, and animals. I remember the stacks of those books—more important to me than what typically occupies a child's mind.

The gifts of wisdom from them—each pearl—lace together and circle my neck in an extraordinary necklace. How extraordinary that a woman denied voting rights in the South until a few years before my birth, and who experienced the strange and prurient cruelties of Jim Crow policies firsthand could plant the seeds for a future far different for her granddaughter. It is not lost on me that who I am today and my journey starts with my grandmothers.

Key Lessons:

1. Standing in one's power means holding grace, integrity, accountability, dignity, perseverance, and courage in balance.

2. Looking to your family roots, to your ancestors, and their wisdom, is a natural way to find the power you have inside you.

Power Summary:

1. The legacy of unsung women in our shared history accentuates the importance of using your voice to not only pay homage but to continue to uplift those historically rendered invisible.

2. Joy, as a form of resistance, is a powerful tool to maintain strength and hope in the face of adversity.

3. Love, resilience, and education can transcend systemic oppression and cultivate empowerment across generations.

Action Steps:

1. Share your voice through creative outlets to inspire meaningful conversations and positive change.

2. Take small, consistent actions to promote fairness and equality, whether by volunteering, mentoring, or supporting organizations that advance social justice.

GLOW TIP

Glow girls, continue to follow the legacy of our brave foremothers, and use your voice to lift others.

Honor the resilience of women who came before us by fostering an environment that inspires learning and creativity, and empowers the next generation.

M B Goodwin

Michele

Author Bio

Michele Bratcher Goodwin is the Executive Producer of *Ms.* Studios and the Linda D. & Timothy J. O'Neill Professor of Constitutional Law and Global Health Policy at Georgetown University where she is also the Co-Faculty Director of the O'Neill Institute for National and Global Health Law. She is the author of the award-winning book, *Policing The Womb: Invisible Women and the Criminalization of Motherhood.* She is the recipient of numerous awards in recognition of her scholarship, research, teaching, and service to civil society.

More info on Michele: https://www.michelebgoodwin.com/

Dedication: I dedicate this chapter to my grandmothers.

Reviews: "Dr. Goodwin's story and unwavering advocacy for women and girls is a bedrock of our organization, and we are deeply grateful for her continued dedication." *Crystal Sprague, Executive Director, Global Girls Glow.*

WE CAN DO HARD THINGS

Mamta Jain Valderrama
FemTech COO, Bestselling Author, Social Justice Activist

———————— • ✸ • ————————

"A girl who uses her voice boldly teaches the world to listen differently." - Mamta Jain Valderrama

———————— • ✸ • ————————

The car beeped and Renu froze. The unrelenting sound rattled her nerves as she reversed out of the garage. Instinctively, she slammed on the brakes, lurching both herself and her granddaughter forward. Her heart raced as her eyes searched the dashboard for answers—flashing lights, warning signs, anything. A yellow symbol flickered, unfamiliar and ominous.

Her hands trembled as she leaned in and squinted at the dashboard. Frustrated and uncertain, she shifted the car into park and stepped out, inspecting every corner for a loose door or a faulty tail light. Nothing seemed amiss.

A Beep That Changed Everything

Her hands trembled as she shut off the engine. She sat still for a full minute, willing her nerves to settle. Reboots fix computers; maybe that would fix the car too? When restarting didn't work, she drove in slow, deliberate circles around the apartment complex. Maybe a warmed-up engine would do the trick.

But the persistent beeping followed her. Defeated, she parked outside of the leasing office. Her hands gripped the steering wheel, knuckles white as her gaze bore through the windshield.

"Naani, let me see."

Her nine-year-old granddaughter, Jiya, unbuckled and crawled into the front. With bony, determined fingers, she opened the glove box and pulled out the hefty car manual. The weight of it dropped onto her lap. Jiya leaned over, her small face just inches from the dashboard.

The Power of a Manual

"Naani, push that button," she pointed to a matching symbol in the manual.

Renu pressed the button and the beeping stopped. The flashing light vanished. Silence filled the car, heavy and sweet.

Renu blinked, her breath catching. "Thank you, Jiya."

Jiya smiled and shrugged as if solving the puzzle was easy. But for Renu, the moment rippled with deeper meaning.

A Lifetime of "No"

Memories stirred—of wearing fluffy frocks and braids slick with oiled hair, of being told, "No, Renu, you can't." Her childhood was full of locked doors, her dreams trapped behind bars of doubt and dismissal. The pattern continued after her arranged marriage in India at twenty-one years old, and even decades later, after she and her husband moved to California.

When she asked for help, her voice would quiver. "The tire is flat," she'd say. "The oil light is on. The car is making a strange noise." Her husband would snap back, "What did you do this time?"

If she offered to handle the problem herself, he replied "You can't. You'll make it worse."

After fifty years of that message on repeat, she believed it. But here was Jiya, fearless and confident, flipping through a manual like it held all the answers in the world.

Lessons from the Next Generation

"I couldn't have done it without you," Renu said, pulling Jiya into her lap. As she squeezed her granddaughter, the embrace melted years of self-doubt.

"Naani, can't is a bad word," Jiya replied matter-of-factly.

Renu stared at her, startled by the clarity in Jiya's tone.

"Mommy and Daddy get upset when I say I can't do something because it's too hard. They make me take deep breaths and try again, even if I get mad. And then they say, 'See? You can do it. You're built to do hard things.'"

Renu smiled, but her chest ached. What might her life have been if someone had told her that? "But how did you know to look in the manual?" Renu asked.

"Oh!" Jiya's eyes lit up. "Our car beeped like that once and Daddy solved it by looking at the manual. Then he showed me what he did."

"You're so smart, Jiya. I'm proud of you."

Jiya beamed. "See? You can do hard things too, Naani. You just need to try."

Renu nodded, a lump forming in her throat. She looked at Jiya, so full of courage and self-assurance, and felt she could still have those things, too.

"You're right, Jiya," she said. "You've taught me something important today. I think I am already a little more like you."

Empowerment is Multidirectional

That night, as I tucked Jiya into bed, she recounted the story with the same steady confidence she must have shown in the car. Her voice was clear and even, as if what she had done was the most natural thing in the world. "Mommy, I could see Naani was nervous. So I helped her." Jiya didn't embellish or linger on her role in the situation.

"It's like what you and Daddy say, 'You're built for the hard stuff.'" Jiya said flatly, as she adjusted her blanket and turned onto her side.

Her words hung in the air as I lay still next to her, marveling at how matter-of-fact it all seemed to her. She didn't realize how profound it was—that a nine-year-old could approach a challenge without hesitation because she had been raised to believe she could figure it out. She didn't see the ripple effect her small act set in motion.

But I did.

Doing the Work of Unlearning and Relearning

That night, I thought about my mom. She grew up hearing "you can't," particularly from her husband, my dad. I also thought about the work I've done to reverse the same doubts passed to me. And

I thought about Jiya, unburdened, and sure of herself. She is doing hard things because we've told her she can. Over time, it's become her truth. In a full circle moment, Jiya helped my mom erase self-doubt, too. Empowerment can flow up, down, sideways, and backward.

As I kissed Jiya goodnight, the weight of the afternoon settled over me. It wasn't just about a beeping car. It was about what happens when we show someone they can overcome challenges.

And when they do, they don't just solve problems—they quietly change the world, one small moment at a time.

Key Lessons:

1. **The Power of Belief**: Believing in someone—especially a child—can create ripples of confidence that transform not only their future but also inspire those around them, breaking generational patterns of self-doubt.

2. **Words Matter**: Positive reinforcement, like avoiding words such as "can't", has the power to shape how someone views their abilities and build a foundation of resilience.

Power Summary:

Together, a grandmother and granddaughter shatter generational cycles of being told "no", replacing these patterns with empowerment and self-confidence.

Action Steps:

Remind one girl in your life that she can do hard things. Whether it's encouraging her to tackle a challenge, teaching her something new, or simply believing in her, your words and actions have the power to create ripples of confidence and empowerment for generations.

GLOW TIP

Global Girls Glow teaches girls to be confident and reminds them that girls can do hard things.

Encourage a girl in your life to take on something new or challenging. Boost her confidence by letting her know you believe in her.

Mamta Jain Valderrama

Author Bio

Mamta Jain Valderrama is a global operations leader and advocate for marginalized communities. A daughter of Indian immigrants, she has worked across healthcare, tech, nonprofits, and publishing to drive social impact. She authored the bestselling novel *A Girl in Traffick*, exposing the horrors of human organ trafficking. She is currently the Chief Operating Officer of Vital Start Health, a femtech behavioral health startup. Mamta also hosts ethical chocolate tastings to raise awareness about labor practices in cocoa harvesting. Known for compassionate leadership, she has led diverse, global teams and managed transformational change with cultural sensitivity and inclusivity.

Contact Mamta at www.linkedin.com/in/mamtavalderrama.

Dedication: For my mom and my daughter, for breaking the self-doubt cycle one empowered girl at a time.

Review: "Mamta's insightful sharing of this powerful and transformative exchange between a granddaughter and grandmother reminds us all how powerful beliefs are, and how believing in someone, especially a child, can make a big impact." *Laura Probst, Social Impact Advisor and CEO Do Good: Make Money.*

A FIRE STARTS TO BURN

Joy Donnell
Writer and Producer

"When bad things stand before you, stand up for the good within you." — Joy Donnell

The Mansion

In 2018, I found myself in an exclusive room in a historic mansion. I'd just been inducted into a cohort called *50WomenCan*, and the group was meeting at the Doheny Mansion, a famous spot in the downtown Los Angeles campus of Mount Saint Mary's University. I'm not typically a joiner, but I gathered with total strangers amid 19th-century woodwork, antique Tiffany glass, and vibrant whiffs of fresh-brewed coffee mixed with powdered pastries. It was a stunningly beautiful place, but I had no idea of the horror that would soon resurface within me—or who I would become on the other side.

My cohort's mission was achieving gender parity in media and entertainment. This felt especially significant because #MeToo had been going viral for four months. We were living something monumental, and everyone in this select group was there to learn how to grow in leadership.

On this particular day, we were workshopping our personal journeys, breaking into smaller groups to share family stories. The goal was to uncover the inflection points that shaped us, and for these insights to unlock hidden reservoirs of leadership potential.

Recalling family history aloud felt strange, like flexing an unfamiliar muscle. I'd grown up around people who could trace their lineage back to the ships you read about in history books. Some had family names etched on the halls of Ivy League universities. My family's story was something else.

My parents were born into Jim Crow segregation, as were their parents. They didn't march with Martin Luther King Jr. or face beatings for registering to vote. But they lived, worked, and created a better life for me and my brother. They moved us into the safest neighborhood they could afford in Macon, Georgia, despite realtors' resistance. We became the first Black family in that part of town. My family history wasn't legendary—it was just a story of survival. I'd never considered it a wellspring of leadership insight. To me, this information was just family chit-chat. I had no idea what to share with this group.

The Sharing

In one of the mansion's many rooms, now reconfigured for modern meetings, five of us sat around a sturdy conference table. We took turns recounting the struggles and triumphs of our ancestors. Someone spoke of immigrating to the U.S. Another painted vivid scenes of the Gold Rush. These were master storytellers—producers and writers who knew how to spin a narrative. My turn was coming.

I planned to keep it light. I'd talk about watching wrestling with my brother and putting him in a headlock, or my mom grilling mangoes and drizzling them with honey, or finally beating my dad at cards. But there was something else lurking in the curved archive of my mind—something I'd never dared to discuss. It felt dangerous, yet insistent.

I parted my lips, ready to describe the smell of fresh-cut grass and chasing fireflies between the pines. Instead, the lurker emerged. It was 1983, around 10 p.m. I was seven years old, rebelling against sleep in the new house we'd moved into just a month prior. Outside my bedroom window, a warm glow flickered. Always prospecting for magic, I thought it might be fairies.

I rose from bed and parted the blinds with my tiny fingers, bracing myself for wonder. Instead, I saw something stranger: a massive cross burning in our front yard, scorching the earth we owned. Someone wanted us to know we weren't welcome. It wasn't just an act of vandalism—it was an act of terror, meticulously planned by neighbors who wanted us gone. They evoked a symbol of the KKK and those who beat, lynched, and killed countless Black people during the days of Jim Crow.

The next day, my parents explained everything to me: enslavement, segregation, and the enduring legacy of racism. I understood their words, but all I felt was rage.

For the next year and a half, our family endured domestic terrorism at the hands of our neighbors. The culprits were eventually caught, but we never spoke of it again. It became a closed chapter in our family's story, survived but unspoken—until that moment in the mansion.

The Discovery

I couldn't believe I was telling this story to a group of women who were still strangers. It poured out as if I was possessed by that seven-year-old me. She arrived cloaked in fury and future, demanding to take up space in a world that tried to make her recoil in fear. My cohort sisters were crying. I cried too, but for a different reason.

At that moment, I realized the necessity of my story. As a child, I had gone looking for magic outside of myself and found hate instead. The discovery was transformative—it was the fuel to look at the magic within me. I embraced self-regard not as the belief that I'm better than everyone else, but as the knowledge that I'm as deserving as anyone else. It wasn't a coincidence that I had been inducted into this cohort to help make a way for everyone, the same way that I'd had to make a way for myself at that tender age.

As I finished speaking, the tears and embraces of my cohort sisters reminded me that this story isn't just mine. It's a testament to resilience, to the strength of those who came before me. Each time I share it, I reclaim it. It has improved the clarity with which I speak and the center from which I draw strength.

I left that room in that noteworthy mansion emboldened by my own history. I walked in unsure of what to say. I walked out knowing my story—and my voice—was a source of magic, not just for me, but for others. Standing for what's right begins with the courage and will to speak truth—even when it burns.

Key Lessons:

Three takeaways arise for me from this journey:

1. **Reclaiming Your Story**: Speaking your truth allows you to take ownership of your narrative and redefine it on your terms.

2. **Building Connection and Empathy**: Using your voice to share vulnerable moments can foster deep emotional connections with others.

3. **Leadership Rooted in Authenticity**: True leadership emerges when you embrace your authentic self, including the challenges that shaped you.

Power Summary:

This chapter highlights that:

1. **Everything you have been through is your journey:** Embrace your whole story as the secret formula that makes you who you are.

Action Steps:

Here are two action steps you can take to carve out space for your impact:

1. **Never doubt the strength of vulnerability:** Others will see the courage required to open up.

2. **Find or create supportive environments:** It can take time but it's worth finding brave spaces where you can share your story and explore its impact. Collaboration and understanding amplify your voice's influence.

GLOW TIP

By believing in the validity of your story, you help other girls believe in the power of their own journey.

When you feel unsure, do it confused. Clarity can come from doing.

Author Bio

Joy Donnell is a producer, writer, and speaker focused on the psychospiritual power of storytelling. Work has been featured in Grist, HuffPost, and Short Edition. Her recent poetry collection, Show Us Your Fire, explores our birthright to self-compassion. Joy speaks internationally about media, equity, and narrative change. She can be found on social platforms under @doitinpublic.

More info on Joy: www.doitinpublic.com

Dedication: For Gayle and your heart-led work that helped this story come forward. To Tabby and Elisa for curating our cohort and championing our growth.

Reviews: "What Joy shares in this story is important. Her words guide us through the process of finding your voice and believing in the authority of your story. It's a lesson in how to figure things out." *Zalika Sapp-Weaver, Entrepreneur, USA*

STEP UP AND STEP BACK

Shruthi Kumar
Founder, Social Entrepreneur, Public Speaker

———————•✺•———————

"Challenging patriarchal norms in a complex culture is a delicate dance between preserving and respecting the beauty of traditional customs while simultaneously questioning outdated norms." - Shruthi Kumar

———————•✺•———————

Arriving at our home in Anna Nagar, Chennai, our little blue car barely came to a full stop before I jumped out, leaving my bags for later. I rushed up the driveway, calling out eagerly to my grandmother, Rajeshwari. "Raj Avva?!"[1] Having awoken from a nap, her groggy but excited response rang through from the kitchen window, "Kanne! Shruthi Kanne!"[2] She opened the door and her comforting presence engulfed me in the biggest hug. I melted into her overweight yet glowing and protective body. She ushered me in and we spent ten beautiful days together.

We shopped for elegant lenghas and sarees, indulged in chaat, and shared quiet moments. She detangled my hair after a shower, fed me my favorite meal of yogurt rice and fried potatoes, and before I left, we filmed a video of her giving me a sweet, old grandma kiss on my cheek—a precious final memory with her.

---

[1] *Avva* is an affectionate term for grandmother in our dialect of the Kannada language.
[2] Tamil term of endearment for children.

32

A few days later, at around 7 a.m., I was jolted awake by my aunt's crying. "Something's wrong with Avva," she said.

A thunderous and rhythmic drum marked the start of the funeral procession. I could feel the deep and ominous bass of the beat in my soul. The priest called for Rajeshwari's grandchildren to accompany her to the graveyard. I stepped forward, only to see the incense sticks handed to a random distant male relative. As per tradition, only *male* grandchildren could attend the burial.

Attempting to remain calm, I insisted to my father that I wanted to go. Why did this distant relative who didn't even know my grandmother, let alone love her like I did, get to participate in her funeral service, and not me? I wanted to be there for the entire ceremony, to see my grandma off to the end.

My father supported me in principle, but warned me that others in attendance would disapprove of me going beyond the village border. My uncle echoed this, noting urban areas like Mumbai had evolved, but our village had remained steadfast in its beliefs.

The men picked up the altar with my grandma's body, and began to make their way to the burial grounds located on the outskirts of the village.

Determined, I joined the procession. The tension grew as we walked through the village.

"Where are you going?" I heard an older woman say behind me, her voice ringing with concern.

I realized the face of patriarchy and misogyny at the root of inequality was not necessarily a man's. What do you do when the face of patriarchy is a woman's?

"You can't go," another woman said.

I kept walking but felt an arm grab me. The oldest woman in our family gripped my face with her frail hands, and pleaded with me to stay. I felt the tears welling up and a giant knot of anger in my throat.

I screamed, "I want to go. I want to go with my grandma. I am going!" As soon as the words left my mouth, I sensed their deep fear for me. "Something bad might happen…" they droned on.

Steeped in superstition, I realized their concerns were about my well-being: menstruation, spiritual possession, my safety, and women's supposed weakness in a graveyard. Despite my desire to challenge these outdated beliefs, I realized that pushing further would only deepen their fears and cause more distress.

We reached the edge of the village, a long stretch of dirt. A gravel road lay ahead, and the men continued on.

I stopped.

I stopped not because I gave up, but because I realized my own stubbornness to participate in my grandmother's burial would create a lifelong fear and worry in the hearts of the elderly women who held such strong superstitions. Their pain and suffering were not worth my own desire to see my grandmother off.

The walk back home was a long and heavy one. I felt like I had failed my grandmother.

Upon returning home, I saw a small silver lamp lit in front of her photo in the pooja (prayer) room, and I learned there was also an important role for the women of the family in honoring my grandmother's death.

While the burial of her physical body was carried out by men, the arrival of her spiritual body was prepared by women. I acknowledged the beauty of the tradition, but simultaneously felt that we all should be allowed to grieve in our own ways.

Back home, I collapsed on the bed, my emotional and physical energy drained. Then my father sat next to me, and began to explain what happened after I turned back at the village border.

For nearly a mile while carrying the altar with my grandmother's body, my father had made an effort to challenge the other men's views. He had explained to them that I had a right to participate. These conversations slowly shifted their perspectives.

While I didn't accompany my grandmother to her final resting place, my insistence had sparked important discussions about gender norms in our community, planting seeds of change.

Key Lessons:

As an Indian-American, I've learned that challenging patriarchal norms in a complex culture is a delicate dance of preserving and respecting the beauty of traditional customs while simultaneously questioning outdated norms.

The women in my family, despite being the enforcers of these traditions, were also victims of the same system. Deep-rooted fears and beliefs are hard to dismantle overnight. This experience reminded me that change is a process, often slow and challenging. Sometimes real change happens through intentional, intergenerational conversations, rather than grand gestures.

My grandmother's funeral was a turning point for me. It reinforced that change is not about imposing one's beliefs on others, but using empathy and respect as tools to find common ground, even with those who have very different beliefs from our own.

Power Summary:

1. **Leverage empathy as a secret weapon in fighting your battles.** Changing deeply held beliefs takes compassion and patience.

2. **A simple conversation can be as impactful as a grand gesture.** Meaningful progress doesn't always require big actions; it often starts with open dialogue and understanding.

3. **Face complexity fearlessly.** Traditions can be meaningful and beautiful, but they should evolve when they uphold inequity or exclusion. It's okay to appreciate the comfort they may provide while also openly questioning the inequalities they may reinforce.

Action Steps:

1. Choose a topic you care about, one that might be controversial in your community, and start a civil, respectful discussion with just one person this week.

2. The next time you are at odds with someone, step into their shoes. Understand why they believe what they believe.

3. Lean into complexity and question simplicity.

GLOW TIP

Individual actions, such as the ones made by Global Girls Glow, are seeds of change—plant them wisely, for the change you inspire will guide and protect generations to come.

Make an effort to understand others' fears and struggles, leveraging empathy to find common ground and make real progress.

Shruthi Kumar

Author Bio

Shruthi Kumar, a recent graduate of Harvard University, holds a Bachelor of Arts degree in History of Science and in Economics with a minor in Human Evolutionary Biology. She is a founder and social entrepreneur, leading menstrual equity initiatives on Harvard's campus and founding a student-led nonprofit focused on preventative mental health education. Shruthi is an internationally-recognized public speaker. Most recently, she was awarded the opportunity to be the 2024 Le Baron Russell Briggs Commencement Speaker at Harvard University. Shruthi is also a United Nations Academic Impact Millennium Fellow and currently co-hosts a podcast on menstruation policy with *Ms. Magazine*.

Website: www.shruthikumar.com

Dedication: To Raj Avva, for your intense kindness and love. To my Kannada-speaking community and Arrupukotai family, for being a home to our shared ancestry and for keeping our language alive.

Reviews: "Kumar has long established herself as a woman unafraid of going against the grain. In this narrative, she dares to offer raw insight into why the modern, empowered woman still grapples with tradition and the urge to rebel against it. A window into her unique but familiar experience with loss, she unravels the intricate layers of equality and empowerment — layers that often seem simple but are anything but. It's at once revelatory and revolutionary in its simplicity!" *Simi Shah Founder & CEO of South Asian Trailblazers, USA*

"Shruthi's story beautifully describes how changes in traditional practices depend on respect and trust across cultures. She brought two distinct cultural patterns to her grandmother' burial. By speaking of her own doubts about a particular woman's role even as she respected it, she opened conversations among both men and women that became a quiet catalyst for change." *Jody K. Olsen, PhD Former Director of the Peace Corps (2018-2021), USA*

"Shruthi's frustration and protests are echoed countless times each day, when women and girls confront cultural constraints that prevent their full participation in society. She demonstrates in this case the wisdom of stepping back from our anger to pursue paths of resistance that may be more successful in the long run, but will require more time for community outreach and education. Long-held views of women as "property" die hard, even when laws recognizing women's rights are enacted, and it may take many generations for principles of gender equality to become more widely accepted." *Judy Norsigian Co-founder and former Executive Director of Our Bodies Ourselves, USA*

SAYING 'NO' TO AN 'EASY YES': HOW I LEARNED TO LET INSTINCT GUIDE THE WAY

Laura Probst
CEO of Do Good: Make Money

———————— • ✸ • ————————

"Your intuition knows what to do. The trick is getting your head to shut up so you can hear." - Louise Smith

———————— • ✸ • ————————

Opening my acceptance letter to one of the top universities in the country was one of the best days of my life. The culmination of years buried in textbooks, striving to get the best grades, the late nights— it all felt worth it. I was smiling from ear to ear as I sat at our sunny kitchen table with my mom and dad, reading the letter:

"Dear Laura,

We are pleased to offer you early admission to…"

I couldn't believe it. An admission to an Ivy signaled that I was one of the best and brightest among my peers. It promised prestige and access; a degree from an Ivy League school could open doors I never knew existed. The invitation to walk the same halls as past presidents and decision-makers not only came with an immense sense of pride, but a swift realization that my future was just beginning. Together, we called our friends and family, and made a plan to visit my future school.

As I strolled through the Ivy League campus I hoped to call home for the next four years, my sense of wonder quickly faded. The buildings looked dark and frigid. I gazed toward my future peers and saw strangers huddled together in the freezing cold, studying sullenly inside library halls. I saw a repeat of striving for academic excellence, grinding, competing—and my stomach churned. How would I have time to discover who I wanted to be and what I wanted to contribute to this world? A shiver went down my spine, and I retreated from this visit with a sense of dread that drowned out the excitement from my family and peers.

My arrival at the University of Virginia a few days later was nothing short of a fluke. I had only applied because *The Insider's Guide to Colleges* boldly stated that UVA students "worked hard and played hard", which reminded me of something my grandpa Stanley said once: "All work and no play makes for a pretty dull life." When I was offered in-state tuition, a major difference from the hefty fees at the Ivy League school, it felt foolish not to consider it, and so we tacked on a visit to the trip.

No, it wasn't the number one ranked school in the country, but as I strolled down the campus sidewalk surrounded by flowers in full bloom and smiling students, a setting once alien to me suddenly felt like my calling. The whoosh of frisbees and the sound of the Dave Matthews Band permeated the air and lit me up inside, and I thought, "This looks FUN!" My toes tingled and a huge wave of calm washed down my back. Between a huge amount of schoolwork, participating in extracurricular activities, volunteering, and working three jobs, I had rarely accessed that fun-loving, adventurous side of my personality that was ready to emerge.

In the weeks following my college visits, my circle of influence was incredulous that I wasn't completely sold on the Ivy. It certainly wasn't a logical path—rejecting early admission to an Ivy felt unheard of. The weight of choosing the less logical path consumed my life, and decision day loomed over my shoulder day and night. At the same time, I had never felt so sure of myself and what I wanted.

When the day came, I stood paralyzed at the mailbox holding two acceptance packets. My hands trembled as I thought of what my parents, my counselor, my teachers, my advisors, and all of the other influences in my life would say if I dropped in the envelope addressed to UVA instead of the Ivy, the school I had proclaimed was my target for all of high school.

But that call to the flowers and the joy that I felt at UVA surged up, and I heard my grandpa's voice and his little chuckle when he said it. Everything inside me said I had to trust my gut, even if everyone would be mad at me and disagree with my choice. So, I did it. I chose myself over prestige and legacy and what I had once strived for, and I put the UVA packet in the mail slot.

I snuck in the side door and crept lightly down the hall to my room, my Ivy packet shoved under my arm. My mom walked in as I shoved the packet in my bottom desk drawer.

"So, did you come to your senses?"

I swallowed hard and said resolutely, "I picked UVA."

"WHAT?! How could you do this?! You are throwing your life away," she said.

There it was. Disappointment. Anger. Rejection. My parents yelled more and stormed off. I was on my own with this choice, and I would have to live with that .

And yet everything good in my life now is directly related to that brave decision I made at 18. I met my best friends. I met my husband. And I had FUN. And I made mistakes I never would have made by only experiencing more of the same. I found and thrived in my work-hard/play-hard balance, and became a version of myself that I am proud of and comfortable with. I made the right choice.

As I write this chapter, I am preparing for upcoming trips to the Dominican Republic, Vietnam, and Malawi to visit children and families I have helped through work I only had the courage to pursue because I found my voice and learned to trust my instinct. It's never gotten easier to quiet the questions and negative voices in my head, but I am grateful for the confidence I have gained in myself. The choice to open new doors in life and see what's on the other side has shepherded me to a life and a career that I absolutely love.

Key Lessons:

1. **Trust Your Instincts Over All Else:** At the time, choosing UVA over an Ivy League school was an unconventional decision.

2. **Embrace Uncertainty:** Facing tough decisions and doubt head-on instead of cowering away from it allowed me to explore my motivations and develop confidence in my decisions.

3. **Seek Personal Fulfillment:** Living authentically and making choices aligned with personal values leads to greater satisfaction. Despite the initial pushback, my decision has led me to make more bold, authentic choices about how to live and do what I know is right.

Power Summary:

1. Live life for you. Enjoy the journey and let go of the guilt

2. Don't let self-doubt and the unknown stop you from taking charge of your life.

Action Steps:

1. Trust your gut. It knows what to do. Sometimes you just need to quiet your mind so you can hear what your gut is telling you.

2. When facing a big decision, visualize the possible outcomes and see which one sits best with you.

3. Be proud of your choices and create the life that you, and you alone, will love. You're the one who gets to live it.

GLOW TIP

Global Girls Glow knows that girls know what girls need and simply helps them find the confidence and power to create the life they want. By trusting your instinct and listening to your inner voice, you are inspiring girls everywhere to do the same.

Listen, check in with your gut, then listen again. Don't be afraid to trust what it tells you.

Laura

Author Bio

Laura Probst is an Emmy-winning marketing and sustainability thought leader, having led impact at The Honest Company and built award-winning purpose and ESG programs for Blackstone PC EQ Office, Paramount, and UNICEF, among others. As CEO of Do Good: Make Money, she has helped dozens of COOs, CMOs and product development teams reduce operating costs, increase revenue, and gain access to additional capital through philanthropy, risk mitigation, and community investment. She works with Madonna, David Ortiz and Mariano Rivera along with several other high net worth individuals on their philanthropic work, and proudly sits on several nonprofit boards.

Website: www.dogood-makemoney.com

Reviews: "What a beautiful reminder of our own innate power to make decisions and live into our full potential with balance and fun. Laura guides us to lean into our intuition even when it's not easy. She shows us that following our gut may lead us into temporary uncertainty. However, the outcome may be a blissful surprise and inspiration to those around you." *Pamela G. Bradley, bestselling author of "Women Who Trust", singer /songwriter, www.pamelagbradley.com*

Dedication: Dedicated to my amazing parents, who continue to always want the best for me and have come to trust my (sometimes unconventional) instincts as well. I love you!

INIOLUWA'S STORY

My Name is Inioluwa, and I'm fourteen years old from Nigeria. I used to think all the girls in my community had equal opportunities until I met Surya.

The first time I saw her, I was excited. My elder sister had just moved away for school, and I felt lonely, longing for someone to share and laugh with. That evening, I overheard my neighbor telling my mother about a maid she had brought in to help with chores. That maid was Surya.

The next morning, I saw Surya cleaning my neighbor's front yard. I tried to say hello, but she barely raised her head, muttering a soft "hi". Over the next two weeks, my attempts to connect with her failed. She avoided eye contact and barely spoke. My hope for a friendship slowly faded, replaced by a deep curiosity about this mysterious girl.

One night, I was jolted awake by screams for help. The voice was unmistakably young. I stumbled through the dark to find my mother sitting in the living room, her face clouded with worry. "Is that Surya?" I asked. She nodded, and my heart sank.

The next morning, I rushed out, eager to see Surya. When I found her, her swollen eyes and red cheeks broke my heart. Her shaven scalp had white patches, and her frailty was painful to witness. I hugged her, and for the first time, she whispered, "I want to go back home."

That day, Surya's voice stayed with me. After school, I saw her sitting alone outside. Without a word, she hugged me tightly and began to cry. Through her tears, she told me everything: how her parents had been promised she would attend school, only to find herself working endlessly from dawn to dusk. Her "madam" beat her for even the smallest mistakes. Surya dreamed of going to school like me, but instead, she was trapped.

I couldn't stop thinking about her. I thought about the love my mother showered on me and the joy I felt in school. Surya deserved that too.

At the next GLOW Club session, I stayed back to share Surya's story with my mentor. With a gentle smile, she assured me we would help. She made a few calls, and the next day, I saw strangers speaking to my neighbor. I prayed silently for Surya's freedom.

Two days later, I saw a woman rushing into our compound. It was Surya's mother. She collapsed into tears the moment she saw her daughter, who was now frail and unrecognizable. As they embraced, I couldn't hold back my own tears.

Surya introduced me to her mother, who thanked me profusely and blessed me. She exchanged contact information with my mom before leaving with Surya.

A month later, my mom handed me her phone. On the other end was a bubbly, excited voice—it was Surya! She told me about her new school and how much she loved being home. Her joy was contagious.

That night, my mom told me how proud she was of me.

GLOW Club taught me how to stand up for others and advocate for what was right. I had found my voice, and with it, I had changed Surya's life.

When Global Girls Glow introduced GLOW Club to my community, I was curious but unsure if I would fit in. Joining the club turned out to be transformative. I discovered myself, learned how to connect with my community, and understood what advocacy truly means. For the first time, I gained the confidence to speak up for myself and others. Attending local summits, I met inspiring girls who shared how they were transforming their communities. Their stories motivated me to advocate for the girls in my own community.

My number one advice to other girls is this: never underestimate the power of your voice, it can spark real change.

Helping Surya made me realize how powerful one voice can be. Today, I'm confident that standing up for others is the greatest way to make an impact.

THREE TIPS ON RECONCILIATION

Meera Gandhi
Author, Philanthropist, CEO

───── • ✸ • ─────

"We are to the Universe only as much as we give back to it." - Meera Gandhi

───── • ✸ • ─────

The Art of Reconciliation

To me, reconciliation is the meeting of dawn and dusk; night and day collide in beautiful harmony and create great splendor in the process. It is natural, powerful, and inevitable. Reconciliation is transformative and healing. It is absolutely necessary for the soul.

As an Aquarian, conflict is very challenging for me. I struggle internally when I have to interact with difficult people. At times, people I've come across do not deliver, do not meet set expectations, or are simply lazy and unethical. I don't judge, and I've learned to exercise love and empathy to resolve conflicts with compassion. It has proven to be the most effective way of reconciling with people and finding ways forward.

An Unexpected Lesson in Grace

In third grade, I attended St Anne's Convent in Pune and was chosen to be part of a 'garba raas' dance for the yearly Prize Day celebrations . We were a group of twelve, and each of us were given two sticks. After every eight beats, we had to turn to the opposite partner and continue the movement. Simple enough.

However, after every fourth turn, I would get confused and either turn too late or turn to the wrong partner. This happened even after a few practice runs.

The teacher stopped the music and called me over to her desk. She asked, "Why are you making this mistake?"

"I don't know," I answered abashedly.

"You have to remember to turn, otherwise, you are wasting our time," she said, and with that, much to my utter shock and horror, she slapped my right cheek very hard. The slap stung me and my eyes filled with tears. "Go back to your place and don't make a mistake this time!" she said savagely.

I mustered all the sincerity and focus possible for an eight-year-old, and began the dance again. When it was time to turn, the teacher walked to my spot, which quickly signaled the correct turn, and soon we completed the dance without any mistakes.

"Once again from the top," she directed, and we did the dance again with no mistakes! Whew!

Biryani, Bonding, and Forgiveness

"Okay, we are done for today. Get your shoes and go back to class," she said.

I got my shoes and then, as I was walking past her, I gave her a smile. She was puzzled and perplexed, but she said nothing. I was halfway out of the door when she called me back.

'Meera, wait, please. Come back. I would like to talk to you.'

Unafraid, I walked back to her, still smiling. She said, "I was unfair to you today. Instead of explaining the step, I slapped you, yet you smiled at me. Why? Most girls would not even have made eye contact."

I answered. "I knew you were trying to get us all to do the dance right. I kept making the same mistake. I kept staring at a bird on the fourth turn. I got distracted and missed the step each time. You slapped me, but Jesus always says that we should turn the other cheek, not respond with hate. Besides, I really do like you!"

The teacher started crying and gave me a hug.

"Who even are you?" she said. "Would you like to come to my home and have a hot lunch with my family today?"

I agreed. We then went down to the principal's office. There, we called my mother for permission. I went to her house, and to this day, I remember what I ate. It was mutton biryani on the floor—boori style—with yogurt and pickles. Hot, spicy, and delicious. Her three children joined us, too. I shared my sandwiches and a red apple with her kids and, as the meal has always stood out in my memory!

On the day of the performance, we danced well and received lots of claps and whistles. The teacher went on to recommend me to lead many other events. The confidence I acquired from this experience helped me take lead roles not only in plays, but also the students' governing body.

We had built a bond over a single incident, and the bond continues to serve me to this day.

This is my earliest recollection of reconciliation. It's pure, powerful, and freeing, and one can never predict what joyful things might follow such a wondrous moment.

Key Lessons:

Looking back on my journey as Founder and CEO of *The Giving Back Foundation*, I've learned that every experience has shaped the way I approach life and leadership. Three key lessons stand out:

1. **Don't let other people's poor behavior dictate yours.** In every challenge, I've learned that how I respond is what matters. Even when faced with negativity or unfairness, I've learned to stay grounded in my values and not mirror the behavior of others.

2. **Take charge of situations, don't let them derail you.** There will always be obstacles, but the key is to take responsibility, stay focused, and not let setbacks define the outcome. I've learned to steer the ship, even when the waters are rough.

3. **Always, take the higher road of doing the right thing.** Choosing integrity is never easy, but I've learned that doing the right thing, even when it's difficult, is the only path that leads to true, lasting impact.

As we move forward, I am filled with gratitude for the lessons I've learned and the growth that lies ahead. Every day, we plant the seeds for a future that will grow far beyond what we can imagine.

Power Summary:

Here are the key takeaways from this chapter:

1. Grace Over Conflict – Responding with empathy and integrity transforms challenges into opportunities for connection.

2. Resilience in Adversity – Staying focused and taking charge of situations leads to growth and confidence.

3. The Higher Road Wins – Choosing to do the right thing, even in tough moments, creates lasting impact and leadership strength.

Action Steps:

1. Exercise compassion: In the words of Mahatma Gandhi, "Compassion is a muscle that gets stronger with use."

2. Practice empathy: Express love and sympathy.

3. Learn to feel unified: Feeling unified is a sure-fire path to reconciliation.

GLOW TIP

This story of reconciliation reflects the core values of Global Girls Glow—compassion, understanding, and empowerment. By turning conflict into connection, Glow encourages young women to use their voices to foster change, create lasting impact, and become courageous leaders in their communities and beyond.

Embrace reconciliation with compassion, for it has the power to heal, transform, and create lasting connections.

Meera Gandhi

Author Bio

International philanthropist and global icon Meera Gandhi has played many roles over the course of her life. As the founder and CEO of The Giving Back Foundation, Meera has travelled extensively in service of the underprivileged. As a former volunteer at Ashadaan, she learnt the joy of self-sacrifice from Mother Teresa herself. As a mother, she raised her three children while successfully managing her philanthropic, business and social engagements.

Meera is the author of *3 Tips: The Essentials for Peace, Joy and Success*; the host of 3 Tips by Meera Gandhi Podcast and The Meera Gandhi Show on B4U Network.

Website: www.thegivingbackfoundation.net

Dedication: This chapter is dedicated to my dear parents, Ellen and Aghee, who continue to love, nurture, and guide me.

Reviews: "The most beautiful moments in life are moments when you are expressing your joy, not when you are seeking it. Blessings in your endeavor to take this message to the world via this book."
- Sadhguru

"Utterly constructive and infused with kindness, wisdom and unshrinking honesty, Meera Gandhi becomes your guide in this life-changing journey of improving yourself, 3 Tips at a time."
- Cherie Blair

"Meera Gandhi's 3 Tips provides practical insights to readers to set out on the path of self discovery. Read it and set out on the journey." - *Shabana Azmi*

GIRLS SCOUT, BOYS DIG: HOW I LEARNED TO CHOOSE COURAGE

Kylie Schuyler, PhD

Mother of 7, Founder and Executive Chair, Global G.L.O.W.,
CEO, Crèmily Inc., a social enterprise brand benefiting girl-
focused organizations globally, Activist, TedX speaker

———————— • ✸ • ————————

"Courage, derived from the French word for heart - Coeur, is the act of pushing through fear so you can be authentically you with all your heart."
- Kylie Schuyler (with gratitude to Brené Brown,
who likely said it better!)

———————— • ✸ • ————————

I grew up in the Pacific Northwest, surrounded by rugged coastline, towering evergreens, lakes and oceans, and endless green moss. As the eldest of four girls, family was vital to me. Some of my fondest memories are of our family clam-digging trips. These adventures were an integral part of our lives—an opportunity to laugh and revel in the simple pleasures of being together as a family.

Our trips began in the pre-dawn hours when my mom and dad would load all of us girls and the clam-digging gear into our old station wagon. We'd bundle up against the cold, still half-asleep, and drive to the beach. There, the air was crisp and salty, dense with fog, and the only sounds were the crashing waves and the chatter of other families gathering for the same purpose. There was something magical about those mornings—being out in the wild before the sun rose, united in the excitement of the hunt.

Once outfitted in our puffy coats, pom-pom topped snow hats, and boots, my sisters, mom, and I set out as "Scouters." Our job was to scour the sand for the tiny dimples that signaled a razor clam hiding below. When one of us spotted that telltale indentation, we'd yell for our dad. He'd rush over with his shovel, racing against the clam as it burrowed deeper into the sand to escape. We Scouters were his cheering section. We watched excitedly as he dug furiously and threw himself onto the sand to reach deep into the hole to snatch the prize. When our dad finally pulled out the clam, he was celebrated as a hero, holding it up like a trophy.

I adored these trips. The cold, the thrill, the camaraderie, and the sense of shared purpose were intoxicating. For a young girl, it felt like magic. But one day, when I was about ten, something shifted for me. As I was scouting for dimples alongside the other women and girls, I looked around and was startled to realize that only men and boys were digging. It struck me. I would never be the one holding up the clam in victory. That role belonged to the boys. Girls scouted, boys dug and triumphed. That was the unspoken rule.

Why couldn't I dig? I was just as strong and determined. I begged my mom to let me try. I wanted to feel the thrill of the hunt, the adrenaline of the chase, and the satisfaction of pulling that clam out of the sand with my own hands.

My mom took me aside, her voice kind but firm. She said, "Kylie, it's not a ladylike thing to do.

And honestly, I don't think you'd be very good at it. Please don't ruin today with your bad mood. Just be happy you're here."

Her words stung. At that moment, I felt a deep sense of unfairness. I didn't have the vocabulary at the time to articulate it, but something inside twisted in protest, and I knew this wasn't right. I didn't want to watch from the sidelines. But instead of pushing back, I swallowed my feelings. I forced myself to be happy because that was what was expected of me.

That day, I internalized three messages I carried for far too many years:

1. *Be ladylike. Don't do anything that challenges that image.*

2. *Don't take risks. You might fail.*

3. *Be positive at all costs. Negative feelings are off-limits.*

As I grew older, these messages shaped how I saw myself and navigated the world. I avoided risks. I tried to conform to societal expectations of what a "good woman" should be. I buried my anger, disappointments, and frustrations, and put on a brave, happy face, even when hurting. On the outside, I seemed fine, but inside, I felt disconnected from myself.

It wasn't until much later in life that I began to question these beliefs. I realized I had a choice. I didn't have to live according to those messages. I could let go of who I thought I was "supposed to be" and embrace who I truly was. It took courage—*emotional courage.* Emotional courage is the strength to share your heart with the world and show up authentically, even when it's uncomfortable or risky.

One moment fundamentally changed everything for me. I volunteered with an NGO that built schools in underserved communities. In 2006, I was in a small rural village in Cambodia on a blisteringly hot day. We were there to celebrate the opening of a new school—the first the village had seen in over forty years. The entire community had gathered, about 150 people sitting amassed on the ground. I stood in front of the crowd, preparing to give a speech, I felt confident and ready.

But then, out of the corner of my eye, I saw her—a little girl standing outside the schoolyard fence. She had her fingers laced through the chain link, watching longingly as we celebrated. Her expression was filled with yearning, and she seemed so vulnerable, barefoot in her little white dress. I couldn't take my eyes off her. She wasn't allowed inside the school; I later learned it was because she was a girl.

Something about her struck me deeply. I didn't understand it at first, but slowly it became clear. She reminded me of my ten-year-old self—the girl on the beach who longed for more, who wanted to be part of the action but was told she couldn't because of her gender. That little girl at the fence was me. And just like her, I didn't want to be confined by societal expectations anymore.

That moment gave me the courage to act. In 2012, I founded Global Girls Leading Our World (Global G.L.O.W.), an organization dedicated to empowering girls to advocate for themselves and pursue their dreams. Today, Global G.L.O.W. works in thirty countries and has reached over 100,000 girls since its inception—girls like that little girl at the fence—and like me.

Looking back, I see how emotional courage has shaped my journey. It allowed me to push past fear, embrace my authentic self, and give my gifts to the world.

Key Lessons:

1. Emotional courage is the strength to share your heart with the world and show up authentically, even when it's uncomfortable or risky.

2. Push through fear and societal expectations so you can live authentically which includes accepting, admitting, and acknowledging your imperfections and vulnerabilities.

3. Build emotional courage by doing one small thing daily that scares you.

Power summary:

When you have the emotional courage to pursue what inspires you, you are a powerful force in the world.

Action Steps:

So, how can you embrace who you truly are? Over time, I've discovered three powerful ways to push through fear and live authentically. Here's how you can start:

1. **Give Yourself an "A":** Appreciate, Accept, Admit, and Acknowledge your imperfections. Try this 21-day challenge to rewire your brain for self-acceptance using "Butterfly Hugs." Every day, cross your arms over your chest and gently tap each shoulder while repeating a meaningful affirmation, like "I am worthy," "I am enough," or "I am confident." Feel the taps resonate in your body.

2. **Face the Dragon:** Build emotional courage by doing one small thing daily that scares you—starting a difficult conversation, taking a risk, or trying something new. With each act of courage, you'll strengthen your resilience.

3. **Dance the Dream:** Pursue what inspires you. For me, that's offering girls tools to advocate for themselves and their communities. To ignite the power of girls to find their voices and lead boldly. What's your dream? Take the first step toward it today.

GLOW TIP

Push past your fears and societal expectations and embrace your authentic self, including your vulnerabilities. If you move forward with emotional courage, you will find you're able to passionately offer your unique gifts to the world.

By choosing emotional courage, we free ourselves to embrace our true selves, share our gifts, and transform our lives and the world around us.

Choose courage! The world is waiting.

Kylie Schuyler

Author Bio

Kylie Schuyler is the Founder and Executive Chair of Global Girls Glow. Operating with the organization's innovative girl-led model, Kylie oversees Global Girls Glow's overall strategy. Collaborating with girls, communities, and the organization's leadership, she helps develop unique programs that address the most critical barriers affecting girls globally.

Kylie is also the CEO and Founder of Crèmily, a social enterprise brand that dedicates 100% of profits to girl-focused organizations, including Global Girls Glow. Kylie serves on myriad nonprofit boards in the U.S. and Asia that focus on women, gender equality, children's education, and mental health. Schools and NGOs worldwide have honored her for her dedication to children's causes. Kylie holds a PhD in Clinical Psychology with an emphasis on Positive Psychology.

Kylie spends her free time on long, slow, meditative runs in the canyons near her California home, where she lives with her husband, seven children, and pint-size puppy, Mabel.

Website: www.globalgirlsglow.org

Dedication: For Jasmine, a Glow Girl from Nepal whose powerful voice at the U.N. at the age of 12 inspired everyone, especially me.

Review: I remember those trips. I remember sand in my teeth and ears. I remember running around on the freezing sand, and, of course, our shoes were wet as we concentrated on the bubbles

and didn't watch the waves. It's hard to be a woman, and this story reminds me how much must be shed to become alive and real. Courage, absolutely. To step out of the dominant paradigm, to become unique, to become yourself takes courage. And it takes stories. Every crisis is a crisis in storytelling. This story reminds me to pay attention to the stories I tell myself—who I am, who I was, what I want to become. You can always change the story.
- *Nina Schuyler, the award-winning author of "In This Ravishing World, and the novel, Afterword."* www.ninaschuyler.com

A JOURNEY OF PASSION AND DISCOVERY

Anu Jain
Entrepreneur / Philanthropist

———— • ✳ • ————

*"I felt myself freeze, a shiver running down my spine. I wanted to make
sure my daughter was well-equipped in STEM and prepared
for the technology-driven future."* – Anu Jain

———— • ✳ • ————

Motherhood

There are moments in life that forever shape who we are, and
for me, one of those moments was the day my daughter,
Priyanka, was born. I deeply love my firstborn son, but when I
found out I was pregnant again, I longed for a daughter—my mini-
me, someone who would be my best friend for life.

My prayers were answered, and Priyanka arrived. As I lay in the
hospital bed, locking eyes with her for the first time, my heart felt
as if it would burst with love. This precious baby, holding my finger
with her tiny hand, was everything I had ever dreamed of. She
quickly became my little doll, filling my life with laughter and joy.

Three years later, when my younger son, Neil, was born, Priyanka
wasn't exactly thrilled about sharing the spotlight. Sitting at the
edge of my hospital bed, tears streaming down her face, she
insisted, "Return the new baby to the toy store!" But soon enough,
her nurturing side took over, and she grew into her role as a big
sister. They became inseparable, playing together and sharing a
bond that remains unbreakable to this day.

As a middle child, Priyanka learned early how to balance relationships. She was both caring and fierce, standing her ground with her brothers and ensuring she was never left behind. One example that perfectly captures her spirit is family Monopoly nights. Her older brother, Ankur, always saw himself as the family strategist, dominating the game with calculated moves. But Priyanka, even as a young girl, refused to be outsmarted. She competed fiercely, negotiating trades and strategizing property purchases. It wasn't uncommon for her to claim victory, proving she was just as sharp and capable as her older sibling. This ability to hold her own in a game of strategy mirrored her approach to life—fearless, determined, and always ready to rise to any challenge.

Priyanka was my best friend and constant companion as a little girl. She filled our home with love, leaving sweet sticky notes and heartfelt poems for me everywhere. One poem, written when she was just nine, still brings tears to my eyes:

"Her soft smile comforts me as I walk into the house after school. She opens her warm and loving arms and gives me a soothing welcome hug. Her silky, curly dark brown hair glistens as the setting sun gleams on it. I gaze at her beautiful and calm eyes and dream that I turn out to be just like her."

Growing Up

But like all teenagers, Priyanka eventually went through a phase where our relationship shifted. Suddenly, I wasn't her best friend anymore. Gone were the warm hugs and hand-holding; they were replaced with eye-rolls and curt words. She spent more time with her friends and less time with me, leaving me feeling left out and lonely. I knew, though, that this was just a phase.

At age sixteen, Priyanka came to me and her dad with a determined declaration: "I've found my passion. I'm going to focus on helping girls improve their lives and have nothing to do with science or technology, so get used to it!" I felt myself freeze, a shiver running down my spine. I wanted to make sure my daughter was well-equipped in STEM and prepared for the technology-driven future. While we admired her ambition and desire to give back, we felt she hadn't yet seen enough of the world to fully understand all her options. Out of love, we decided to push her—not to change her path, but to expose her to opportunities she hadn't considered.

We arranged for her to attend Singularity University for four weeks during her summer break, where she would learn about neuroscience, genetics, artificial intelligence, and robotics. Priyanka resisted, rolling her eyes and saying, "You don't even hear me! I don't want to go there!" But we struck a deal: if she went with an open mind and still felt the same afterward, we would support her dreams wholeheartedly.

Four weeks later, Priyanka came home, standing tall in the kitchen with her usual confidence. "Mom, Dad, I've made up my mind," she announced. We held our breath as she continued, "I want to study neuroscience and genetics." Surprised and thrilled, we asked her what had changed. Her response moved me deeply.

"I care about girls' education and health," she said. "But now I realize that science and technology are the tools I need to make a real impact. No one ever taught me that in school. STEM isn't just about memorizing facts—it's about solving the problems I care about most and using technology to scale the solutions."

In that moment, I saw my daughter not just as my little girl but as a future leader, ready to use her talents to change the world. She had discovered that science and technology weren't destinations—they were tools to pursue her passion for helping others.

Key Lessons:

That experience taught me a powerful lesson as a mother. Sometimes, our role isn't to tell our children what to do but to show them possibilities they might not see on their own. By pushing Priyanka, we didn't just help her discover her true calling; we also gave the world a remarkable mind working to improve lives.

Today, at just thirty years old, Priyanka is the Founder and CEO of Evvy, a women's healthcare company focused on closing the gender health gap. She is a confident leader, using science and technology to drive meaningful change, and she continues to inspire me every day.

Parents, when your children dig in their heels too early, don't be afraid to nudge them toward discovery. Girls, don't get stuck on one career path at an early age without exploring more. The world benefits when young people find passions they didn't even know existed. And as a mom, there's no greater joy than watching your child shine in ways you always knew they could.

Power Summary:

1. Motherhood: I loved being a mom and best friend to my daughter.

2. Challenges: Having a teenage daughter was no easy task. I was no expert. Reflecting on my belief system and knowing when to push back.

3. Lessons learned: Don't give in to your child's passion right away, but encourage her to explore beyond her current dreams and think big.

Action Steps:

Here are three simple action steps that you can do to inspire your own bravery and tap into your inner brilliance:

1. Embrace being a mom and enjoy the journey.

2. Be proud of your daughter and inspire her to think bigger at every step of her journey.

3. Say it with me, "Dream BIG and Be BOLD. STEM is POWER"

GLOW TIP

Don't get stuck on one idea. Be fearless and cultivate a love of learning throughout your life. Learning never stops!

Don't limit yourself—explore new opportunities, think big, and know that you have the power to shape the future with your unique voice and ideas.

Anu Jain

Anu Jain

Author Bio

Anu Jain is an entrepreneur and philanthropist focused on advancing women globally through innovation and technology. She is Head of Women's Health at Viome, a company leveraging gene expression to optimize one's health. Anu invests in startups prioritizing women's health and leads their family foundation supporting Girls / Women / Education and Health. A proud member of Women Moving Millions, she also founded the $1M Women's Safety XPRIZE and advises the UN Foundation's Girl Up. With a global upbringing and degrees in business and economics, Anu lives in Medina, WA with her husband, and is a proud mother of three successful entrepreneurial adult children.

More info on Anu: www.linkedin.com/in/theanujain/

Dedication: To my daughter Priyanka, Founder and CEO of Evvy, whose brilliance inspires me daily. To all mothers nurturing future leaders, and to every girl with dreams—may you always believe in your limitless potential to create change.

Reviews: Anu provides valuable insight on helping girls overcome limiting beliefs. By exposing her daughter Priyanka to diverse knowledge frontiers, she empowered her to expand her horizons. This key principle applies across all areas and seasons of life.
- Namita Purohit, Leadership Coach, Eastern Wisdom and Western Psychology

THE MAGIC IN THE MISSING

Kelsey Chittick
Author | Speaker | Life Coach

———————•✹•———————

"This is a story about choosing joy and gratitude, not only in the good times but especially when times are gut-wrenchingly hard." - Kelsey Chittick

———————•✹•———————

The Call

I had twelve grief books on my nightstand, seven lasagnas in my refrigerator, two sobbing kids—and one dead husband.

It was a cold, dark afternoon, and I was in bed wearing mismatched Target pajamas, staring at my ceiling fan. As the fan went around and around, I tried to focus on one paddle as a sort of weird mental game, but I kept getting distracted by all the dust. "Someone should clean that," I thought, but I couldn't move. I had no energy. No hope. The only thing I could do was lay there thinking, *We are so screwed.*

Three days earlier, while I was 6,000 miles away on a spiritual retreat, I received the call we all fear. I had just gotten out of the beautiful Jamaican water and remember thinking, *Everything has changed. I'm a new person now.* When I walked into the hotel lobby, still dripping wet, I looked at my phone and saw a call from an unknown number. I answered and heard a deep voice, "Hello, I'm Dr. Smith from UCLA. Are you Kelsey Chittick?" I was confused. "Yes, what is this about?" There was a long pause. "I'm so sorry, Mrs. Chittick. We did everything we could, but Nate didn't make it." Suddenly, the world went quiet, and time stood still. "Wait, what? What do you mean?" I asked.

"I mean that your husband is dead."

On 11/11/2017, at 11 a.m., my incredibly gifted husband—lover of all people, NFL football player, Super Bowl Champion, and father to our nine- and twelve-year-old children—died of a massive heart attack at a trampoline park in front of his kids. He was forty-two.

The Decision

I felt like I'd been dropped onto a different planet. Nothing made sense. The pain was too big to comprehend. But as time went on, moments of clarity and an inner calm began to surface. I toggled back and forth between heartbreaking grief and extreme gratitude. Often, I thought, *I'm going insane.* For a while, I wasn't sure if we would make it. The days were so hard, yet some mystical and magical moments had begun to arrive also.

I started to pay attention to everything. The good and the heartbreaking.

The first miracle happened on the last plane back to the States. I had taken the last available seat and immediately went into shock. I couldn't breathe. As I began to hyperventilate, I felt someone put their hand on my shoulder. I looked up and saw a beautiful Jamaican woman in a colorful dress. She looked me in the eyes and said, "I don't know what you're going through, but I know people are praying for you. Slow your breathing down, baby girl, and know angels are all around. You are stronger than you think."

The Acceptance

As my breathing slowed, I nodded and squeezed her hand. Suddenly, I realized I wasn't alone. I closed my eyes and heard a voice in my head say: *Kelsey, your kids just lost their dad. They are NOT going to lose you.*

That mantra became my North Star.

The first three months were brutal. The pain of missing him was so physical, but around month three, I felt something changing. One morning as I cried in the kitchen, my daughter walked in. It was a few days before her tenth birthday. "Mom, are you okay?" she asked. I looked down at my dirty robe, greasy hair, and swollen eyes. "No," I said. She grabbed my hands with desperation, "Mom, please. I don't want you to always be sad anymore. I just don't want everything to be so sad anymore." In that moment, I realized we had gone from a joyful life to complete devastation overnight. It was time to start a new path of healing and hope.

We were desperate for happiness but didn't know how to balance it with the pain. "Alexa, play

'Three Little Birds' by Bob Marley," I told our Amazon speaker. My daughter looked stunned—there hadn't been music in our home for months. As the music began, she started to smile. For the first time in months, we had a little space from the pain. From that moment on, we began to create and recognize small moments of joy—and walk toward them.

Key Lessons:

This story is not just about death and dying. It's about love and life. I've learned we can't control everything, and hardships will show up. But what defines us is how we respond.

Here's what I know now:

1. **Gratitude** – The only feeling that overcomes grief is gratitude.

2. **Healing** – There is no "end" to grief, but there can be a transformation in how we live with it. Death often teaches us the most important lessons about life.

3. **Bravery** – The Universe favors the brave. Trust you are guided and guarded by something bigger than yourself.

Power Summary:

I believe life is filled with tough times and magical moments. During hard times, the most important thing we can do is surround ourselves with great people and strong tools. The tools I leaned on at the beginning are the same ones I use today:

- **Meditation**: Sit quietly and center yourself.

- **Movement**: Walk in nature

- **Music**: Turn on your favorite songs and feel alive.

- **Magic**: Trust in life's bigger plan.

The bigger the pain, the more life-changing the lesson. Often, we can't experience great joy without great sorrow. When we begin to look at our hardships with the same reverence as the good moments, life becomes spectacular.

Action Steps:

1. Close your eyes and think about something you're afraid of. Now say out loud: *"I can handle anything that comes my way. I have everything I need to thrive."*

2. Reflect on a hard moment in your life that turned out to be a gift. For example, you didn't get into the college you wanted, but you ended up in the perfect place.

3. Look in the mirror and say: *"The Universe favors the brave, you are not alone"* three times. Feel the support and love rise within you.

Glow Tip

Global Girls Glow is dedicated to empowering young girls and women worldwide, helping them recognize their strength, feel supported, and understand that their stories and

voices matter. These resilient young women, who have overcome significant challenges, are poised to become the leaders of tomorrow, with their efforts paving the way for future generations.

Instead of praying that nothing bad ever happens, pray that whatever comes your way, you have the strength, courage, and faith to not just survive it, but thrive.

Kelsey Chittick

Author Bio

Kelsey Chittick - Certified Life Coach, Podcaster, and Best-selling Author of "Second Half - Surviving Loss and Finding Magic in the Missing."

Kelsey has been featured on "The Doctors", The Drive with Peter Attia, and speaks around the country about grief and resilience. She loves yoga, walks by the beach, and spending her time with her two children.

More info on Kelsey: www.kelseychittick.com

Dedication: To Jack and Addison may you always remember that you were born from a beautiful love story. You two are the reason I will always live in gratitude and joy.

Reviews: "Kelsey's journey through loss teaches us how to handle hard times. The tools she introduced, along with her relentless focus on gratitude, shows us how challenging moments can also be beautiful and empowering." *Karin Ross, Executive Vice President Government Affairs, USA.*

"Kelsey has a way of taking a gut-wrenching loss and turning it into a beautiful story of love and perseverance. Through her experience, she teaches others how to lead with gratitude and find a way to write their own ending." *Michelle Keldorf, President, Marin Acquisitions, USA.*

FROM DREAMS TO ACTION: MY TRANSFORMATIVE JOURNEY FROM INDIA TO ENERGY INDUSTRY LEADERSHIP

Nandini Sankara
Vice President, Marketing and Brand Strategy and Spokesperson

———— • ✦ • ————

"Confidence is essential in life. Believing in YOU and the differentiated value YOU bring to any situation makes one stand out in a crowd."
- Nandini Sankara

———— • ✦ • ————

A Humble Beginning in Mumbai

I grew up in the bustling city of Mumbai, India. My parents are progressive thinkers who provided me and my sister with an extraordinary foundation. From our kitchen chats to community events, they emphasized the importance of resilience, education, and giving back. Unlike many women in my community who faced societal constraints, my sister and I were encouraged to follow our passions, find our voices, and build lives according to our own rules.

My *AHA!* moment came when I was nine. I was watching TV and noticed that men played dominant roles in society as doctors, leaders, and decision-makers, while women were in supporting roles or homemaking. I knew I had to do something to change this narrative.

Challenges in Carving a New Path

I arrived in the U.S. as a young adult to pursue my master's degree with no financial safety net or support system. Self-reliance became my mantra and I told myself every night as I stared at the sky, *I will MAKE IT.* I spent my first year here sleeping on an air mattress on a friend's floor. Everything I owned fit into a suitcase and my weekly splurge was a Three Musketeers bar!

It was on one of those nights that I vowed to use my degree to change my life and never spend another night sleeping on someone else's floor. I was determined to succeed and give back to everyone who supported me along the way.

Resiliency in Action: Transforming Adversity into Success

My professional journey has been nothing short of metamorphic. After earning my MBA in Management Information Systems, I held leadership roles at Sealed Air, Aetna, and Pitney Bowes, all of which taught me invaluable lessons about resilience and innovation.

In 2017, I joined Suburban Propane to lead marketing and brand. My mission was clear: modernizing an iconic brand while honoring its century-old heritage. With only ninety days of experience in the energy sector, I led a brand refresh, introducing innovative marketing strategies and earning buy-in from stakeholders across the company. It wasn't easy, but it became one of the proudest accomplishments of my career.

I found fulfillment in founding and leading the SuburbanCares platform, which supports hyperlocal nonprofits. This work allowed me to combine my professional expertise with my passion for giving back, creating an impact far beyond business metrics.

Conclusion: A Legacy of Change

Reflecting on my journey, I'm incredibly proud of how far I've come. From a curious nine-year-old in Mumbai to a leader in the energy sector, my path has been shaped by courage, determination, and a commitment to making a difference. Whether it's advocating for women's education, mentoring young professionals, or reshaping a brand's identity, I've learned that resilience and purpose can leave an indelible mark on the world. And I hope my story inspires others to embrace their individual passions and journeys with courage and conviction.

Key Lessons:

1. **Embrace challenges as growth opportunities:** Every obstacle is a chance to discover new strengths and achieve greater things. This mindset translates into my career and leadership style, where rejection and obstacles are part of the journey. I view setbacks not as endpoints but as catalysts for innovation, fueling my determination to find creative solutions and drive progress.

2. **Lead with purpose:** Success isn't just about personal accomplishments; it's about paving the way for others. A cohesive and cooperative team makes or breaks any endeavor. Working together towards a common goal, where every employee acts as a brand ambassador, is crucial. By fostering a culture of shared vision and mutual respect, I empower individuals to see their roles as integral to the bigger picture, amplifying their contributions to collective success.

3. **Give back:** True fulfillment comes from helping others unlock their potential and succeed. This can be done through building meaningful relationships with team members advising interns straight out of college, and even acting as a sounding board for family and friends. Giving back not only strengthens communities but also creates a ripple effect, inspiring others to pay it forward and nurture future leaders.

Power Summary:

Born and raised in India, I was fortunate to grow up in a household that strongly encouraged independence, education, and ambition—values not always afforded to women in my community. From a young age, I recognized gender disparities in leadership and set my sights on breaking barriers.

As a young adult, I moved to the U.S. alone to pursue higher education, facing financial hardship and the challenges of adapting to a new culture. Despite these difficulties—sleeping on an air mattress and sacrificing meals to make ends meet—I remained steadfast in my commitment to education as the key to transforming my future.

With resilience and determination, I earned my MBA in Management Information Services, going on to hold leadership positions at global corporations, including Sealed Air, Aetna, and Pitney Bowes. In 2017, I joined Suburban Propane as their Vice President of Marketing and Brand Strategy, leading a major brand refresh and launching the SuburbanCares initiative, which supports local nonprofits in addressing food insecurity, veterans' issues, and education.

Action Steps:

If you're looking to make an impact, here are three steps to get started:

1. **Find your voice—and use it!** Speak up in meetings, share your ideas, and believe in the value of your perspective. For me, this means striving for stronger advocacy for gender equality, challenging stereotypes and correcting biases. By confidently expressing our unique viewpoints, we pave the way for more inclusive and innovative conversations that drive meaningful change.

2. **Seek mentors and allies:** Surround yourself with people who inspire and support you. Those who feel supported are able to give the best support to others. Strong relationships built on trust and mentorship not only fuel personal growth but also create networks that uplift entire teams and communities.

3. **Stay curious and courageous:** Keep learning and pushing boundaries, even when fear threatens to hold you back. Have the courage to use the word "no" as a complete sentence. This type of openness and confidence will help you gain support from important stakeholders. This mindset fosters resilience and empowers you to take bold actions that align with your values, building credibility and earning respect from those around you.

GLOW TIP

Embrace Challenges as Stepping Stones – Every obstacle is an opportunity to grow. Whether you're starting fresh in a new country, tackling career roadblocks, or pushing for change, resilience and purpose will carry you forward. Stay committed to your vision, adapt, and turn adversity into fuel for success.

Embrace bold leadership, break barriers, and inspire change. Your ambition has no limits—OWN it.

Nandini Sankara

Author Bio

Nandini Sankara is Vice President, Marketing and Brand Strategy, and Spokesperson for Suburban Propane Partners, L.P. An advocate for women and diversity, Nandini is the first female person of color officer at the company. She led Suburban's brand refresh and the launch of its renewable-energy platform. A world traveler fluent in four languages, Nandini supports causes like the Save Elephant Foundation and serves on the Northern NJ Red Cross board. With over 20 years of leadership experience at global firms like Aetna and Pitney Bowes, she's a featured speaker at events including SXSW and WLPGA.

Website: www.linkedin.com/in/nandinisankara

Dedication: To my parents- Even from half a world away, you remain the voice of reason and courage that fuels my success.

Reviews: "Nandini's journey reflects her strong leadership qualities, characterized by courage, resolve, and a commitment to inclusion. Her exceptional skills and talents not only fuel her success but also inspire those around her.

As a female leader in historically hyper-competitive global industries, Nandini's impact is evident throughout her career delivering long-term benefits for the organizations she has served. Whether exponentially increasing a brand's visibility in the marketplace, building a strategic marketing engine from the ground floor, or creating entirely new operational systems, Nandini's legacy is rooted in leading real-world, long-lasting business results leaving her mark on organizations worldwide.

Beyond her professional achievements, Nandini is deeply passionate about fostering cultures of inclusivity. Her inherent ability to bring together diverse perspectives from all areas of her experience encourages collaboration while empowering others along the way.

Nandini exemplifies a leader who, with unwavering courage and determination, not only drives transformative business outcomes but also fosters community of inclusion. She is a role model for generations of female leaders to come!" - *Doreen Domask, Digital Media & Marketing Sales Executive Driving Growth for Global Brands*

"Nandini has done a wonderful job of refreshing and energizing the nearly-100-year-old Suburban Propane Brand with philanthropic and smart marketing endeavors. Also, it's been a pleasure to watch her establish and mentor an excellent team of professionals within her oversight accomplish bigger things year after year." - *Julie Kahn, President at Julie Kahn Communications.*

HUONG'S STORY

People often say, "Family is where love resides." For many, family is a safe haven, a place of protection and care. But for me, it hasn't been that way.

I was born into a family with both a father and mother, along with an older sister and younger brother. When I was very young, my father had an accident and was only given a 1% chance of survival. Miraculously he woke up, but he could no longer work. The burden of daily life, combined with her own misfortunes, led my mother to take everything out on my sister and me.

I often wondered, "Do parents who assert authority through fists and punishment ever realize the harm they are causing to their children?" One of my greatest fears was witnessing my parents argue and fight, and the crashing sounds of objects being thrown.

Every fight left me feeling hopeless, powerless, and depressed. Over time, this created a cycle of violence that became ingrained in my subconscious.

"If I die, will you and Dad stop fighting?" That's something I actually said. It was the first thing I uttered after enduring countless moments of physical and emotional abuse. My mother seemed to believe in the saying, "Spare the rod, spoil the child," but it felt like that applied only to my sister and me. Many times, I watched her express affection for my younger brother, while I felt sad and unloved.

My childhood was filled with loneliness, sadness, and constant fear. When my mother was upset, instead of comforting her, I felt the need to distance myself. One time, I asked her if she was in pain, and she scolded me harshly. Since then, I never dared approach her again. The bond between us grew more distant with time.

Living with my family meant living according to my mother's emotions. If she was upset, I felt fear; if she was happy, I felt safe. Over time, I withdrew into darkness, losing the will to speak or fight back. Eventually, my parents divorced, and I moved to the countryside to live with my paternal grandmother, leaving behind that abusive environment.

Living in a new place made me more shy and introverted. For years, I battled anxiety and relied on tranquilizers to cope, especially throughout my school years. As a child witnessing and experiencing violence, I gradually believed it was my destiny. I thought every family had its dark side, and dreaming of a safe, loving home was a mere illusion.

Then one day, I saw my sister being violently abused right in front of me—her body bruised, trembling, and fear deeply etched in her eyes. I asked her, "If you could have one wish, what would it be?" Struggling to speak through her shaking voice, she replied, "I just wish for a place to come home to without fear…"

Her words struck me like a knife to my mind. I realized the helplessness and fear in her eyes mirrored what I felt during my own experiences of abuse.

In that moment, I understood that what I went through was not my fault, nor was it something anyone should ever accept. Love isn't about enduring pain or sacrificing oneself to keep a family together. A true family should be a safe place—free of shouting, pain, or control.

Perhaps having endured the depths of pain, I yearned for a real family, one filled with love and a home to return to. I believed this small hope could bring light to my life.

One day, while sitting in the corner of my room feeling sad, I received a notification on my phone from Thao, a GLOW Club member, encouraging me to accept the invitation to join the club. At first, I felt a bit skeptical, fearing I wouldn't fit in or that I was too weak to step out of my shell. But a faint sense of hope stirred within me. "What if this could be a chance for change?" I thought.

I accepted the invitation to join GLOW Club. That night, I couldn't stop wondering about the first day—whether anyone would talk to someone as shy as me, or if they would judge or criticize me. I was filled with mixed emotions.

The first day at GLOW Club was a beautiful day. Stepping into the classroom, my heart raced with anxiety and excitement. During the session, I sat in the corner, feeling shy as the room was full of lively, kind people who eagerly approached to talk to me. But I couldn't utter a single word—I just stared blankly at the wall, lost in my thoughts.

Then, I realized that my companions had also faced many hardships in life, and they were willing to share their stories. I vividly remember Thao confidently sharing how she overcame fear to pursue her dream of becoming an actress, and Ngan recounting the journey of a family member who overcame hardships to build a career. Many others shared their journeys, too. In that moment, I suddenly felt less alone—everyone here understood and created a safe space where fears could be acknowledged and supported.

Thanks to the incredible environment at GLOW Club, I began to believe in their message, and I experienced significant changes in my journey of self-discovery. I learned to think positively, believe in myself, and express my opinions to challenge outdated stereotypes. It marked a turning point in my life.

That day, after school, I received a call from Lan, a 9th grader I had met on social media. She was sobbing uncontrollably, saying she didn't know how to deal with what was happening in her family.

Lan shared that whenever her parents argued, she felt terrified. Her father frequently yelled at her mother and sometimes even threatened violence. Lan felt deeply anxious, scared, and alone. She couldn't talk to anyone about it.

I explained to Lan that domestic violence isn't just physical abuse but also includes emotional violence, such as yelling, threats, or loss of control. Feeling scared during parental arguments or being stressed about their relationship are signs of an unsafe environment. I shared that in Lan's situation, it was crucial to stay calm and protect her emotional and mental well-being. I encouraged her to share her feelings with her parents or a trusted adult, such as grandparents, uncles, aunts, or teachers. I emphasized that it wasn't her fault for feeling anxious or afraid in such circumstances, and she had the right to be protected from its negative effects.

I assured Lan that I was always available to listen when she needed to talk. Lastly, I told her that seeking help is a courageous act and the first step toward change. Thankfully, Lan later connected and spoke with her parents, and she no longer felt as worried.

What I've learned at GLOW Club has greatly helped me resolve my own issues, offer advice to other girls, and share my story with confidence and clarity. Through their supportive community, I learned how to express my voice unapologetically, using my experiences to inspire others and make a positive impact.

The opportunity to contribute to this anthology, *Voices for Impact*, has allowed me to reflect on my journey and amplify my message with courage, compassion, and authenticity. By sharing my story, I've not only found my voice but also connected with others who are striving for change, creating a ripple effect that encourages others to speak up and make a difference.

Witnessing the suffering caused by family violence left me feeling heartbroken. Every time I saw the wounds on my sister's body, I felt deep emotional pain. But I realized silence and endurance were not solutions.

By sharing my story, I've helped others become aware of domestic violence and how to address it. This not only breaks the silence but creates a strong support network for those in similar situations.

I've learned that domestic violence should never be endured in silence. We must confront it, share our experiences, and seek help from the community. Everyone has the right to live in a safe and loving environment. When the community speaks up and takes action, we can reduce domestic violence and help victims regain peace.

No one should live forever in fear. Domestic violence is never acceptable. Sometimes, speaking up is the first step toward a freer, more peaceful future.

Don't be afraid or feel alone because you deserve respect, love, and safety. Share your story with someone you trust, because "Your voice has the power to change lives."

When one person speaks up, they can become a light guiding others to escape violence. We each have a unique "voice," but not everyone finds it easy to recognize and use it. To discover and empower your voice, follow these three steps:

First, "Listen to Yourself." Ask yourself: "What do I truly want?" "What are my values?" Understanding yourself helps you focus on your authentic voice.

Second, "Dare to Speak and Express Your Opinions." Fear of judgment can hold you back, but sharing your thoughts helps clarify your values. Start with small conversations and express your opinions. Don't fear being yourself, because only by speaking out can you discover the strength in your voice.

Finally, "Practice and Persevere." Using your voice takes time and patience. Practice regularly—through journaling, discussions, or speaking in groups. Practice builds confidence and clarity. Also, listen to feedback from others to grow.

No one deserves to live in fear or pain from violence. You have the power to overcome and live a happy life. If I can do it, so can you! Finding and using your voice isn't easy, but by listening to yourself, daring to express yourself, and practicing consistently, you will unlock the strength your voice holds.

Remember: Your voice matters. Let it be heard.

WHEN WORDS FAIL YOU

Dr. Lindsay Ruiz, Ed.D

Founder | Transformation Leader | Startup Mentor

———————— • ✸ • ————————

"It took me quite a long time to develop a voice and now that I have it, I am not going to be silent." - Madeleine Albright

———————— • ✸ • ————————

For the first thirty-three years of my life, I navigated the world oblivious to the dangers of having been raised in a very dysfunctional family. The walls I built to protect myself became maladaptive coping mechanisms that carried me into adulthood. They were my armor, but they were also my cage.

My voice—my truth—became collateral damage.

I remember one particular afternoon, lying on my therapist's couch. It was like something out of a movie, except there was nothing cinematic about the terror I felt. My marriage was collapsing, my job felt suffocating, I felt deeply broken inside, and I couldn't articulate why. I was crying inconsolably, paralyzed by fear, dreading the thought of going home that evening. My therapist, powerless to offer an immediate path forward, looked at me with a mix of compassion and urgency.

"Oh my God, Lindsay!" she said, *"You have completely lost your voice."*

Her words cut through me like a scalpel, exposing the raw truth I had been avoiding. It took her five seconds to hold up that mirror and ten years for me to begin to see the real reflection of myself.

That night, when the session finally ended, I sat in my car and Googled:

How does someone know they have lost their voice?

Just like the *Wicked* song says, something "changed within me" that night; something was never the same again. After that profound realization in therapy, my voice eventually began to return. First, in a poem I titled "Speechless". From there, my recovery grew into a leadership journey. Over the years, I committed to understanding the unique power of my voice to inspire and mobilize others, as well as to speak truth to power in moments of profound injustice.

Countless times I've stood for what's right, often alone, speaking up for those who couldn't expose cruelty or suffering themselves. I've learned that our inner core expresses our deepest virtues, and that using our voice is humanity's most powerful tool for change.

Losing Your Voice Is Not Just Metaphorical; It's Physical

By now, you've probably been encouraged to use your voice, speak your truth, and take up all the space that you deserve. By every means possible, make that your ultimate quest!

But be prepared.

There will be times when reaching new heights feels distant and uphill. When the weight of what's unspoken becomes unbearable, your overwhelming feelings and strong convictions are trapped like a knot in your chest, a lump in your throat, a weight on your shoulders. Your body knows what it wants to express, but your mind blocks the way. You want to speak, to cry out, to be heard, but nothing emerges. You sit in silence, your voice buried so deeply it feels lost. You swallow the words, hoping they'll disappear, but they don't.

I know this feeling intimately. Don't worry, you'll break through.

You will realize that staying silent serves no one: not yourself, the people you love, or the world you want to impact. You'll soon learn that self-censorship is a form of self-abandonment. Silencing your truths allows others to define who you are, what you believe, and what you deserve. Speaking up is an act of rebellion against that abandonment. It declares: *I am here. I matter. My voice matters.* It's terrifying, yes, but also liberating.

To the Girl Who Feels Voiceless

If you feel like your words refuse to come out, I see you. I've been you. I've felt the ache of staying silent when everything inside is screaming for me to speak. I want you to know that you're not trapped forever. Your voice is still there, waiting for you to reclaim it. Sometimes it's fear: fear of rejection, judgment, or retaliation. Other times, it's conditioning: the belief that you must stay small, quiet, or agreeable to be accepted. It's okay to be scared. It's okay to stumble.

The only thing that isn't okay is giving up on yourself.

I want to inspire you to dream bigger, reach farther, and challenge the norms you've been too scared to confront. Losing your voice is not the end, but the beginning of a transformative path toward shedding your fears and embracing your power to speak truth in all of its forms:

Reclaiming your identity and standing up for what you believe in.

Using your voice on your own terms.

Challenging dysfunctional systems and defending the marginalized.

Supercharging your ideas for justice and change.

Transforming shame into pride, authenticity, and love.

You will find your voice again, and then once more. Not the voice the world has told you to have, but the one that has always been yours. And when you do, the world will shift. It will shift because of your bravery, your truth, and your refusal to stay silent. You will be the leader of a lifetime!

Key Lessons:

1. The world will always have opinions on who you should be and how you should act. Trust your gut and listen to your intuition, it's your truest source of wisdom. The moment you feel the urge to censor yourself is when you must speak. Silence in the face of conviction betrays your true self.

2. Find your cause and stand, even if it's terrifying. The world has enough bystanders, don't join them. Even if you stand alone, stand.

3. Your voice doesn't need perfection; it just needs to be yours. Speak, even if it's messy, shaky, or uncertain. Clarity comes through action.

Power Summary:

1. **Silence Equals Self-Abandonment.** Staying silent when you feel the urge to speak betrays your authentic self. Speaking your truth is a rebellion against self-abandonment.

2. **Your Voice is Enough.** Your voice doesn't need to be perfect, it only needs to be yours. Speak, even when it's messy, because clarity will come with experience and practice.

3. **Your Words Are a Catalyst for Change.** Use your voice to challenge dysfunction, stand up for justice, and create a ripple of transformation.

Action Steps:

1. **Start Small.** Practice speaking up in low-stakes situations. Share an opinion casually or express your needs to a trusted friend.

2. **Reframe Beliefs.** Identify one silencing thought (e.g., "I'll be judged") and replace it with: "My voice matters, and I deserve to be heard."

3. **Take a Stand.** Pick a cause you care about and advocate for it. Post your perspective online or speak up in meetings.

GLOW TIP

Global Girls Glow is committed to helping young women and girls discover the power of their voices and embrace their truths. Just as I found the courage to reclaim my voice, Global Girls Glow empowers girls to speak up, share their valiant stories, and lead the way for other girls. By amplifying your voice, you create space for others to rise. When one voice shines, it lights the path for many.

Humanity needs what only you can say. Your voice has the power to shift the world.

Lindsay

Author Bio

Dr. Ruiz is the Founder & CEO of human as usual, a generative scaling studio for early to late-stage startups and mid-market companies that aim for ambitious revenue goals, while honoring every dimension of the human experience.

As an executive leader, Dr. Ruiz led global change and transformation initiatives for Fortune 500 and major growth brands, in industries ranging from advertising & healthcare/ biotech, to technology, retail & consumer goods/ services, executing high-visibility initiatives around the complexities of organizational change and scaling up.

Doctor in Education in Applied Behavioral Sciences, Business Coaching & Change Management, Startup Mentor, Workplace Psychological Safety Advisor, Thought Leader/ Speaker.

Website: www.humanasusual.com

Dedication: To the girl who lost her voice. You, me, us. May she accept that her voice will heal the world. May she be free to speak her truth. She's loved.

Reviews: "Lindsay's essay about losing and finding one's voice resonated deeply within me. It tells the stories of so many women I know who did not have the comfort of a childhood full of the love, security and acceptance we all wish for. It also speaks to my own vulnerability and empowers me to say 'yes' to my own voice and to the possibility of transforming my own life, the lives of others and ultimately the world we live in for good." - *Samira Weiss-Bouslama, M.Sc., Coach, Facilitator and Master for Ecology, Austria*

"Lindsay's authenticity in sharing her story has been incredibly inspiring. She has touched the lives of many who were confined by limiting beliefs, showing them the courage to break free and guiding them toward becoming their best selves and reaching their highest potential." *Elizabeth Bacon, Chief Information Officer, United States*

"Lindsay's story is a powerful reminder of the transformative journey to reclaim one's voice. By sharing her vulnerability, she inspires others to confront their fears, embrace their truth, and speak with courage. Her actionable lessons—trusting intuition, speaking through fear, and standing up for what you believe in— empower readers to honor their authentic self and create meaningful change. This piece encourages us all to see our voices as tools for authenticity, leadership, and collective transformation. Thank you Lindsay for sharing these tools and inspiration." *Melissa Santoro, Finance Senior Executive, Board Director, Leadership Faculty, United States*

HOW I LOST MY VOICE IN THE HUSTLE
– AND FOUND IT AGAIN

Jennie Blumenthal
Leadership Expert | Bestselling Author | 2x Entrepreneur

———————•✻•———————

"If the quality of life is the quality of your relationships—with others for sure, but especially with yourself—how could I stay?" - Jennie Blumenthal

———————•✻•———————

It was a Tuesday morning in September when I walked away from my twenty-year corporate career. I was a Partner at a leading global consulting firm, running a $250 million business, managing 300 people, and helping Fortune 100 companies hit billion-dollar growth strategies. My role put me on planes several times a week, and my company was positioning me for a big new title that year. I was on an upward trajectory as the only woman on my business unit's leadership team. My career had never been bigger, nor my star brighter.

But that was all on the surface. Deep down, in a place I didn't like to think about, I felt like this job was slowly killing me. The passion I once had helping C-level executives grow into new markets and run huge transformations was replaced with managing headcounts and profit margins, plus the reality of raising two elementary schoolers with a husband who had his own big career. I would schedule my client meetings and flights around bedtimes to make sure I was there to sing them to sleep before dragging myself back to the computer to send one last email.

On top of the relentless pace, I was feeling lonelier than ever as a female leader and working mom with a focus on innovation and growth. My days involved working alongside accountants and risk managers with fundamentally different approaches, who didn't always welcome my perspective or ideas. I had worked so hard to climb this ladder, I expected it to be worth it. To feel GOOD. So if it didn't, I told myself, maybe the answer was just around the corner—maybe I needed to put my head down and tell myself to feel happy.

Facing Reality

And then the pandemic hit. Planes were grounded, and despite the fear across the world, in the world of our house, we took up tennis and puzzles and did pandemic walks. I thought maybe this was it: I'd finally figured out how to manage this big job and still have the closeness with my children and husband that I craved. But the whole facade came crashing down one night when my ten-year-old brought me dinner after a day full of calls with my teams in my makeshift home office. I apologized for how busy I must seem but shared that I was happy I was here at home and not on a plane, and that we'd had fun that summer. He looked at me and cheerfully told me the truth that I needed to hear:

"Yeah, the summer has been great! I mean, you've been on Zoom calls every day, all day, but at least I've gotten to see you on the weekends!" And that did it: something inside me cracked. The illusion that I could simply hustle harder to be happy fell apart at that moment.

From Hustle to High Impact

By that point, I was in extreme burnout and had no idea. So I left. To save myself and my family more than anything else—but what came next is what taught me to truly find my voice. I threw myself into understanding how I could have fallen into burnout, and not even known it. I dove into research and read fifty books, interviewed 300 executives, studied neuroscience in business, and slowly began to unlearn what I thought leadership was and learn how to lead myself intentionally. I compiled those insights into a bestselling book and launched a leadership development company based on an approach I named Corporate Rehab—to shift from surviving your career to thriving. I now get to work with global teams full of executives and entrepreneurs in reconnecting with themselves, growing intentionally, and unlocking their potential.

Finding my voice during the process of writing the book and launching a company on my own was less about having the perfect story, and more about tapping into the truth about what I felt and thought. That meant resisting the urge to share only what I thought everybody wanted to hear. Over time I had learned that when I spoke up—vocalized what I was thinking, feeling, or experiencing —it wasn't always appreciated. So I stopped. I rounded off my edges and I toned down my words to make sure that they landed softly on the ears of the powerful. I climbed the corporate ladder to the next rung, and then the next. But the higher I got, the emptier I felt. What did I really think underneath that perfectly designed presentation and meticulous appearance?

What did I really feel, as I was flying away from my children to close one more deal?

The quieter I became throughout the process of looking inward at my life and choices, the louder the drumbeat insisting that there had to be more to my life. So I began to tell the truth about how I felt to my coworkers, to my husband, and to myself. It was terrifying. I had to face the truth about abusive behavior, toxic bosses, and the unhealthy patterns I learned in childhood and carried into adulthood. There was broken glass everywhere. But there was freedom on the other side.

I wanted to tap into my real voice, my authenticity—but after years of people-pleasing, I had to constantly resist the learned behavior of trying to make my truth and my voice acceptable to others. To wrap it all up in a bow and serve it up as something safe for others to consume. It took telling my stories without any polish, getting them out of my body and into the world, to get me started.

And then? Others began to respond to my vulnerability in telling the truth. "Me too. I feel seen. I feel heard." It was then I truly realized the power of using my voice, not only for myself but to give others permission to speak and share their stories, too.

Key Lessons:

When I look back at this journey, a few main ideas come to mind:

1. You have unique gifts and perspectives based on your life experience that can help others.

2. Sharing your story by telling yourself the truth can help you feel unburdened—and gives permission for others to feel seen and do the same.

3. Perfect is the enemy of good enough. Start sharing it even if it has raw edges. Those who are meant to hear your story will gravitate towards you.

Power Summary:

Let's recap the highlights of this story:

1. Make sure you're making decisions with your life based on your own expectations and definitions of success instead of other people's.

2. Getting still and quiet can be the best way to channel your inner wisdom.

3. Tapping into your own voice requires you to LET GO.

Action Steps:

Here are three simple action steps that you can do to inspire your bravery and tap into your inner brilliance:

1. Think back on your own life's story. What are some of the highs and lows?

2. What are some of the things you wish you could share with others?

3. Start sharing your perspectives and personal story to inspire those around you.

GLOW TIP

Global Girls Glow is passionate about amplifying the voices of young women and girls worldwide. Over the past few years, they have empowered thousands of girls to share their stories and become courageous leaders, and sharing what you think, in the way only you can, is one way to tap into your own courageous story.

Take the first step towards reconnecting with the story that is uniquely yours—I'm cheering you on!

Jennie Blumenthal

Author Bio

Jennie Blumenthal. A former Fortune 100 exec turned entrepreneur, Jennie is passionate about helping leaders reach the next level of leadership on their own terms. After spending 25 years in Corporate America managing multi-million dollar growth strategies, Jennie left her partnership in a global consulting firm to launch her own leadership company. Based on the concepts in her bestselling book, *Corporate Rehab: Ditch the Hustle Culture and Thrive Again*, her work has impacted 15,000 globally and helps leaders achieve their potential and thrive in the future of work. She lives in DC with her husband, kids, and puppy.

For more information on Jennie's work: www.corporate-rehab.com

Dedication: For Kevin, Jackson and Avery, for reminding me that I know myself best, for every woman who shared her story in these pages, and for those who carry their stories alone.

Reviews: "If you're an executive or aspiring leader - this is the leadership story you didn't know you needed." - *Dr. Bobbi Wegner, CEO of Groops, USA*

"We need to create cultures to retain the best leaders. We can't do that without women." - *Shelley Zalis, CEO, The Female Quotient, USA*

"Drawing from her own story of hitting the wall in our American overwork culture, Jennie has given a voice…to millions of women and caregivers who've left or been forced out of the workforce, exhausted, overwhelmed, overworked, and looking for more in their lives and work." - *Brigid Schulte, NY Times bestselling author of "Overwhelmed", USA.*

WHY DO MEN BENEFIT FROM GENDER EQUALITY?

Gerardo Porteny Backal
CEO & Founder, Grupo Educathion, former consultant: Global Youth Engagement UN Women, Founder and Chairman of the board of Pink Life Against Breast Cancer A.C. and Young Minds for Gender Equality A.C.

———————— • ❋ • ————————

"Achieving gender equality benefits both men and women, therefore we must collaborate as part of the solution." - Gerardo Porteny Backal

———————— • ❋ • ————————

Starting Out In the Nonprofit World

I was a nineteen-year-old Mexican man in London, standing in front of a packed theater in Covent Garden, about to deliver my first TEDx Talk. I was confident in my impact, but I never imagined how profoundly this event would transform not only my worldview but my entire life.

The event, TEDx Covent Garden Women, featured twelve speakers. I was going to talk about Pink Life Against Breast Cancer A.C., the nonprofit I founded at age sixteen. Naively, since it was a female-focused event, my nineteen-year-old self thought everyone was going to talk about breast cancer. To my surprise, I was the only one addressing that issue, while everyone else spoke about ways to achieve gender equality.

Men Should Also Fight for Gender Equality

This was my first exposure to the topic. Like many young men, I had no formal education on it. Growing up, my parents, Eduardo and Tammy, worked as a team, raising me and my sisters, Paola and Melissa, in an equal environment. I couldn't imagine that outside my "bubble," 3.5 billion women faced barriers to equality.

After the event, I hugged my mother and sister in relief. But soon, reality set in. That night, I couldn't sleep, thinking about how much worse the world would be if women like them were denied opportunities. These achievements benefit all of us as a society—not just them or even just women, but every single one of us, including men, young men, and boys. I knew I needed to take action, and my first step was to educate myself on the subject.

I soon learned that it was important to support women—economically, socially, politically, and in many other spheres. As I continued my research, I discovered that for the past two hundred years or so, several brilliant women have led the fight against gender-based discrimination and inequality, achieving countless victories that paved the way for us today. I also found that in the past 30 years, several pioneering men have organized themselves to address issues such as toxic kinds of masculinity and gender roles across different cultures.

To my surprise, not much had been done to foster collaboration between women and men to be part of a solution that benefits everyone: achieving gender equality. Inspired to take action, I soon started my second 501(c)(3) nonprofit organization, *Young Minds for Gender Equality*. I immediately began reaching out to other young men and women around the world who had shown their support for gender equality on social media. Before long, we created a network spanning over 52 countries, where young men and women led educational and awareness initiatives in their cities to show other young people how important it is for both genders to achieve equality.

The HeForShe Movement

I was fortunate enough to catch the attention of the United Nations, particularly UN Women. The special adviser to the Executive Director invited me to a meeting at their headquarters in New York. That's where I had the privilege of meeting Madame Phumzile Mlambo-Ngcuka, the Under-Secretary-General of the United Nations and Executive Director of UN Women from 2013 to 2021.

In 2014, she shared with me her vision of creating a global solidarity movement called HeForShe. Its goal was to invite men and young men around the world to be part of the conversation and the solution for gender equality. It was an honor to be invited to serve as the Consultant for Global Youth Engagement for UN Women and to be part of the amazing team that developed and implemented this solidarity movement. But I never imagined the reach that HeForShe would have until I listened to Emma Watson, the brilliant goodwill ambassador for UN Women.

On a September night in the General Assembly Hall of the United Nations, she delivered her now-legendary invitation to men around the world, asking them to remind themselves: "If not me, who? If not now, when?" Since that moment, HeForShe has grown into a major force for good, inspiring countless men worldwide, including political leaders, university presidents, CEOs, and men from all walks of life, to commit to taking specific positive actions in support of gender equality within their sphere of influence.

I wish I had an entire book to share with you all the things I learned and the amazing people I met during this incredible journey. But since I only have this chapter, I've decided to share with you a foolproof formula to convince any man in the world that gender equality benefits them. As you'll see in the following story, this realization can be both powerful and transformative.

When I lived in New York and worked at the United Nations, I was invited to deliver the keynote speech at the annual retreat of a nonprofit that I hold very dear to my heart, called MCW Global. During the event, I had the opportunity to meet a brilliant young man named Alex. We had a conversation that ultimately led to this formula.

Alex was unconvinced that gender inequality impacted him as a young man. So I asked him: *What if your amazing mother were not only able to receive equal pay as other men in her company for equal work, but also gain a promotion and the recognition she deserves for her work, regardless of her gender?* Surprised by the question, Alex responded that it would be amazing for his mom and, as a matter of fact, she was already looking for a promotion.

I followed up with another question: *If your mom got a promotion and achieved equal pay for equal work, would that impact you at all?* Alex immediately answered: *Of course! I'd have more time to spend with my mom, and our household would have a greater income, benefiting me, my dad, my sisters, and, of course, my mom.*

At that moment, Alex realized an inevitable truth: gender equality benefits us all.

I leave you with this story as inspiration so you can convince other men—and the men in your life—that when women and girls win and can achieve their full potential, it doesn't just benefit them. It makes all of us, as a society, stronger.

Key Lessons:

1. **Collaboration is Key:** True gender equality requires men and women working together to create solutions that benefit everyone.

2. **Education is the First Step:** Understanding gender inequality and its effects is essential for creating change. Start by learning about the issue and encouraging others to do the same.

3. **Youth Can Drive Change:** Young people, when empowered, can play a crucial role in advancing gender equality through education, advocacy, and collaboration across cultures.

Power Summary:

Gender equality benefits everyone, including men. Collaboration between men and women is essential for achieving sustainable progress. Engaging men as allies in gender equality movements, such as HeForShe, demonstrates the power of collective action in breaking down stereotypes and promoting inclusivity.

Education is a critical first step. Empowering young people as advocates creates a ripple effect, fostering a future where equality benefits all.

When women succeed, society thrives.

Action Steps:

1. **Educate Yourself and Raise Awareness**

   ○ Learn about gender inequality and how it impacts society as a whole.

   ○ Share your knowledge to inspire others to join the conversation and take action.

2. **Support Equal Opportunities**

   ○ Advocate for equal pay, promotions, and recognition for women in your workplace and community.

   ○ Challenge and address discriminatory practices wherever you see them.

3. **Engage Men as Allies**

   ○ Involve men and boys in the fight for gender equality by showing how it benefits everyone.

   ○ Encourage discussions that challenge stereotypes and promote inclusivity in all areas of life.

GLOW TIP

Create empathy to raise awareness: Connect gender equality to personal experiences. If a man struggles to see how gender inequality affects him, encourage him to reflect on how the achievements of women in his life—like his mother, sisters, or daughters—positively impact his well-being. Show that when women have equal opportunities, it benefits not only them but also their families, communities, and society as a whole. This personal connection can be a powerful starting point to gain their support for gender equality.

Gender equality isn't just a women's issue—it's benefits everyone. Educate yourself, challenge stereotypes, and advocate for equal opportunities in your community and workplace. Together, we can create a more inclusive, equitable world where everyone thrives. If not you, who? If not now, when?

Gerardo Porteny Backal

Author Bio

Gerardo Porteny Backal is the Founder and CEO of Grupo EducatHion, leading 21 online schools focused on democratizing education through technology. His platforms, including Monedu (Personal Finance) and Nano MBA (Business), empower students worldwide. Gerardo has collaborated with institutions like Universidad Anáhuac and organizations such as UN Women, where he was part of the team that developed the HeForShe movement as a Global Consultant on Youth. He founded Young Minds for Gender Equality and Pink Life Against Breast Cancer. Recognized as a "Global Visionary of Education," Gerardo is a sought-after speaker with 4 TEDx talks and holds a B.A. Magna Cum Laude from NYU and post graduate studies from Oxford University and Harvard University.

Review: "Gerardo's text is a powerful call to action, showcasing how gender equality benefits everyone, including men. Through personal stories and practical steps, he highlights the importance of education, collaboration, and empathy in driving change". - *Dr. Pilar Mora, PhD, Author and Creator of the "MEISI Method".*

Dedication: A mi mamita, gracias por enseñarme lo que las mujeres pueden lograr por la sociedad.

To my mom, thank you for teaching me what women can achieve for society.

Link: www.grupoeducathion.com/english

FROM BLENDING IN TO INSPIRING CHANGE

Kylie van Luyn
Psychotherapist, Coach and Human Rights Consultant

————————— •✱• • —————————

"Every setback is a seed of strength, every challenge an opportunity to grow. Embrace your journey. You are destined for greatness." - Kylie van Luyn

————————— •✱• • —————————

Growing up, I struggled to use my voice. Secondary school was marked by bullying that destroyed my confidence and left deep scars on my self-esteem. For most of those years I felt invisible, as if my thoughts and voice didn't matter. The negative words and actions of others convinced me that blending into the background was safer than standing out. It's hard to explain the lasting impact that bullying has, but it's a shadow that followed me well into my adult years, making me second-guess my abilities and dim my light.

And then, just when I thought I had my feet firmly on the ground, life threw me another curveball. At twenty-two, I lost my darling mother to cancer. The trauma of losing her was shattering. Instantly, my world went dark and stayed that way for some time. My mother had been my safe space, rock, and greatest cheerleader. In the weeks and months following her passing, I felt untethered, drowning in grief that seemed all-consuming. But amidst the emptiness and darkness, I promised to make her proud.

I wanted to honor her memory by empowering others, particularly women and girls, to find their confidence, use their voices, and live their truths, just like she had done. My mother was a pillar of strength; she was warm and kind, but no-nonsense. She lived her life out loud. I wanted to be just like her.

This healing journey was neither linear nor easy, but it taught me resilience. I found my purpose through this grief and pain—to uplift, inspire, and support girls. My mother had always believed in my ability to make a difference, and I clung to that belief, even on the most challenging days.

The birth of my daughter sixteen years ago further solidified my mission. When I held her in my arms, I felt an even stronger sense of responsibility—not just to her but to the world she would grow up in. She inspires me daily with her strength, curiosity, and boundless potential. I knew that to make the world a better place for her and other girls, I had to start by fully stepping into my power. This determination led me to launch my coaching and consulting firm four years ago, ironically, on Independence Day, the day before my Mother's birthday.

I had been an executive for over twelve years and found mentoring women and girls the most rewarding part of my job. I wanted to build a company that allowed me to do more work empowering girls at school and impacting aspiring leaders. But the journey hasn't been without its challenges. As a woman in leadership, I encountered sexism, pushback, and resistance. I had to fight to be heard in rooms where my voice was undervalued and overlooked.

Throughout my career, I've had the privilege of working with girls from all walks of life. From designing coaching programs to mentoring young women on their career journeys, I've seen firsthand the resilience and strength that girls possess.

One of my proudest moments came in 2019 when I was named a finalist in the Australian State Business Women's Awards for empowering women from refugee backgrounds across Australia. But I didn't feel worthy when I stood on stage to accept the award. I felt self-conscious and questioned whether I deserved this accolade I'd earned.

Key Lessons:

Imposter syndrome has been a constant companion for most of my life. As a coach and consultant working with women and girls, I've often had to remind myself that my work speaks for itself. The voices of self-doubt have been loud, but the thousands of voices of the women and girls worldwide that my team and I have supported—sharing how their lives have changed—have been louder.

Early in my entrepreneurial journey, I learned that influencing legislation was the most powerful way to impact and achieve real, sustainable change. I was up for the challenge! Over the past two years, I have worked tirelessly to advocate and influence legislative change across the USA to ensure all American workers are protected from workplace psychological abuse and harm, and I have designed and delivered programs globally to empower girls and women who have been victims of gender-based violence and harassment. Everything I do is infused with the lessons I've learned and the belief that every girl has the power to rewrite her story.

Two years ago, I connected with Global Girls Glow and volunteered as a mentor and speaker. Their values and mission resonated deeply with me. Global Girls Glow is undoubtedly the go-to organization for empowering girls and young women and amplifying their diverse voices to drive meaningful change. It is an honor to volunteer with such a phenomenal, purpose-driven organization.

Power Summary:

My daughter has asked me why I do what I do. My answer: I believe in a world where every girl feels seen, heard, and valued. A world where we don't have to fight for our place at the table because we've built our own. A world where using our voices isn't an act of courage but a natural extension of who we are.

I am driven by the belief that change is possible. Too many girls feel forgotten, invisible, and unworthy, like I did. It hurts my heart, but it also fuels my passion. I've made it my mission to open ears, hearts, and minds. To remind girls that they are powerful beyond measure and that their voices matter.

Action Steps:

I hope my story inspires you to believe in yourself, feel the fear, and do it anyway! I've learned that the things that once made me feel different or unworthy now fuel my purpose and passion to make a difference in the world. Pain, grief, and self-doubt can either hold us back or propel us forward. I choose to let them propel me forward. Think about what will propel you towards success.

GLOW TIP

Over the past decade, I have almost said no or backed out of amazing opportunities because of fear or lack of confidence. Had I not shifted my mindset, regained my confidence, and had the determination to push through the limiting beliefs, I would have missed out on life-changing experiences with phenomenal people. Now, my motto is, "Feel the fear and do it anyway!"

In 2023, I was honoured to be named one of the Top 10 Influential Female Entrepreneurs, and in 2024, I was a Women of Influence Finalist. These milestones remind me of the possible impact of pushing past fear and self-doubt to stand in your truth.

There is so much more to accomplish, so many more lives to impact. Together, we can elevate and inspire the next generation to live life on their own terms. When one girl finds her voice, she paves the way for others to do the same.

Kylie van Luyn

Author Bio

Kylie van Luyn is an international speaker, best-selling author, award-winning coach, and human rights consultant. As the Founder of Elevated Coaching & Consulting Global, Kylie brings over 15 years of international expertise empowering girls and women to overcome challenges and step into their greatness. A Harvard Business School graduate, accredited psychotherapist, and NLP Master Practitioner, Kylie blends her diverse qualifications with her passion for unlocking human potential. Recognized globally, Kylie was named among "The Most Influential Women Leaders To Watch in 2024" and awarded CEO Today's Human Rights Consultant of the Year. Her work inspires purpose, resilience, and impactful change worldwide.

Website: https://www.elevatedconsulting.net

Dedication: For my darling daughter Sienna and my beloved late Mum, my inspiration to be the best woman I can be every day. And for girls everywhere.

Reviews: "The best way to learn is to stand on the shoulders of giants. Well, for those who have had the privilege of meeting Kylie face-to-face will know she is tall and Amazonian like. A true beautiful giant. She is a giant in running a business with integrity and a giant in identifying her client's blind spots and supporting them to overcome their limiting beliefs. A giant coach with heart.

What I value most is Kylie's authenticity: She walks the talk and practices what she preaches. She is efficient. On time. And shares her lessons learned with a generous spirit. Her passion for raising women to their full potential is spectacular. Every minute spent with Kylie is a lesson in kindness, compassion and challenges me to step up. Kylie, thanks for being the most generous and awesome mentor!" - *Theresa Loo*

"Kylie, you have been such an inspiration to my personal, career and family life. Your compassionate heart and spirit has been able to make me see light above all barriers that I was facing. I am now seeing life and my new career as the best change ever and it's all because of your inspirational leadership that goes above and beyond. Forever grateful." - *Maria Giaourtas*

"Every time I deliver your female purpose-built workshops, I am always reflecting, channeling the amazing creator that is you. Often I will pause during my delivery and speak of you to the women and tell them how you live to inspire women and change their lives somehow.

I feel myself driving the message in the same way and love watching their engaging reactions and interactions…leading from the front is a saying I believe you inspired us with.

I have taken back what is in my control and found a way to quieten the noise in the background so I can focus on the bigger picture that life has in store for me. We are always on our journey - sometimes we don't always know what that looks like or how this will take shape… however, control what you can control and have a purpose (this is you inspiring me). Don't lose sight of that picture/goal and strive forward; this is where I am, and let me tell you, this feels very empowering.

Whatever the future looks like for me, I have truly learned so much from you, and your purposefully written programs inspire me to take courage in the future no matter what." - *Cherrylee Maybury*

Conclusion

Join us in empowering the next generation of unstoppable voices. Together, we can make the world a place where every girl has the confidence to raise her voice and change the world.

Throughout this anthology, we have heard from bold, courageous, and compassionate women on their personal experiences with finding their voice, overcoming obstacles, and unapologetically sharing their message with the world. These stories, each unique and powerful in their own right, reflect the universal truth that when women—especially young women— dare to raise their voices, they can spark change in ways that ripple through communities, countries, and cultures.

As we wrap up this powerful collection, it's important to remember that there are still too many girls around the world facing systemic barriers to education, opportunity, and self-expression. Too many girls are told to be quiet, shrink, conform, or stay in the shadows. These girls deserve to be heard. They deserve to share their messages with the world without fear of judgment or rejection. They deserve to know their voices matter.

The stories in this book provide a helpful guide for how all of us— leaders, activists, educators, parents, and mentors—can create environments where girls feel safe, supported, and encouraged to embrace their full potential. Each chapter has highlighted the importance of clarity, courage, and compassion, and these are the qualities we must continue to cultivate in the next generation of girls. But there are so many global challenges to making this dream a reality.

This is where Global Girls Glow comes in. Our mission is to uplift, mentor, and empower girls from all walks of life to share their voices boldly and shine unapologetically. We provide mentorship programs, leadership training, and a platform for girls around the world to become powerful advocates and confident leaders. Through our work, we are equipping young girls with the confidence to tackle the world's most pressing challenges, from climate change to period poverty to education. But we can't do it alone.

This book is just one piece of the larger movement we're building. We invite you to join us in this important work. To invest in the future of girls. To ensure that they are heard. To make their voices matter. Your support—whether through donations, partnership, or joining us in advocacy—makes a profound difference. By supporting Global Girls Glow, you are building a brighter world: A world where girls lead.

The next generation of advocates, change-makers, and visionaries are ready to rise. It's our job to help them speak out with unapologetic confidence. The time is now. The girls are ready. Will you answer the call?

Crystal Sprague
Executive Director, Global Girls Glow

BONUS CHAPTER

14 Tips to Share Your Message with Courage, Clarity and Compassion

Sharing your voice can feel intimidating, but it's one of the most powerful tools you have to create change, inspire others, and live authentically. In this bonus chapter, the authors of *Voices for Impact* share their most useful tips to help you find the courage to speak up, the clarity to share your message effectively, and the compassion to connect with others meaningfully.

These straightforward and actionable insights are designed to empower you to make a difference—whether in your personal life, workplace, or community.

Encourage big dreams – *Anu Jain.* Don't give in to your child's passion right away, but encourage her to explore beyond her current dreams and think big.

Engage men as allies in gender equality – *Gerardo Porteny Backal.* Gender equality benefits everyone. Involve men in conversations and show them the power of inclusivity.

Tell yourself the truth – *Jennie Blumenthal.* Start by being honest with yourself. When you own your truth, you create space for others to do the same.

Find brave spaces for your story – *Joy Donnell.* Surround yourself with people who encourage you to speak your truth and embrace the power of your story.

Embrace your imperfections – *Kylie Schuyler, PhD.* Give yourself an "A" – Appreciate, Accept, Admit, and Acknowledge who you are. Self-acceptance is the key to confidence.

Turn fear into fuel – *Kelsey Chittick.* Name a fear that holds you back. Say out loud: "I can handle anything that comes my way. I have everything I need to thrive."

Own your voice and power – *Kylie van Luyn.* You are more powerful than you think. Trust that your voice matters and that your story can inspire change.

Trust your instincts – *Laura Probst.* Facing uncertainty? Take a deep breath and trust your gut. Bold decisions lead to growth.

Empower the next generation – *Mamta Jain Valderrama.* Identify one girl in your life and remind her: "You can do hard things." A simple affirmation can shape her confidence.

Lead with compassion – *Meera Gandhi.* Show kindness daily. Small acts—listening, helping, encouraging—create lasting impact.

Express love in everyday moments – *Dr. Michele Goodwin.* Love is in the little things: a smile, a handwritten note, sharing a meal, or teaching someone to read and write.

Speak up, even if it's messy – *Dr. Lindsay Ruiz, Ed.D.* Start small. Share your thoughts in a meeting or voice an opinion with a friend. Each step strengthens your voice.

Have courageous conversations – *Shruthi Kumar.* Pick a topic you care about, even if it's controversial, and start a respectful discussion with just one person.

Find your voice and use it – *Nandini Sankara.* Speak up in meetings, share your ideas, and believe in the value of your perspective.

By applying these lessons, you have the opportunity to not only find your voice but also amplify the voices of those around you. Remember, even the smallest step can create ripples of change.

Now it's your turn. Take these tips and use them to speak your truth, advocate for what matters, and connect with others in profound and meaningful ways. Let this book be a reminder that your voice matters, your story matters, and your courage has the power to impact the world.

Take the leap of bravery!

Sincerely,

The Authors and Team of "Voices for Impact"
Organized by Global Girls Glow

BARRIERS

I know you're looking at me
But do you really see me?
Are you threatened?
Am I suspicious?
Because I look different

I know you're probably judging me
But these whispers are misleading

I feel a shaking in my bones
See your eyes cold as stone
If I run… will it ever change?

Barriers… Barriers
Pushing through barriers
I gotta change the way I see you
If you're ever gonna see me

Barriers… Barriers
Pushing through barriers
We gotta love a little harder
We gotta hold each other stronger

I know you don't hear your words
Or the way that they hurt
As they're playing
Over and over and over again in my mind…

As my children find me
Laying on the floor
Tears streaming down my face
Trying to open up my heart to you

Barriers… Barriers
Pushing through barriers
I gotta change the way I see you
If you're ever gonna see me

Barriers… Barriers
Pushing through barriers
We gotta love a little harder
We gotta hold each other stronger

Can we find the footsteps in the dark
To where there's nothing but love

Barriers… Barriers
Pushing through barriers
I got to change the way I see you
If you're ever gonna see me

Barriers… Barriers
Pushing through barriers
We gotta love a little harder
We gotta hold each other stronger

Pushing through barriers
Pushing through barriers

Breaking down barriers
Breaking down barriers

Music written by Izdihar Jamil and Drew Lawrence
Music composed by Drew Lawrence
Sung by Izdihar Jamil

To hear the song, go to:
https://www.izdiharjamil.com/songs

SCAN ME

GET INVOLVED

Global Girls Glow is a 501(c)(3) organization that mentors girls around the world to become powerful advocates and confident leaders. Its signature program, GLOW Club, is facilitated by trusted local mentors in more than 30 countries, including the United States, providing girls with a safe space to express themselves as they learn to advocate for themselves and the issues they care about.

Visit globalgirlsglow.org/readmorestories to help unlock the potential of the next generation of leaders or

Contact info@globalgirlsglow.org to invest in the power of girls today!

SCAN TO GET INVOLVED

www.ingramcontent.com/pod-product-compliance
Lightning Source LLC
Chambersburg PA
CBHW071807090426
42737CB00012B/1987